The Online Student's User Manual

Everything You Need To Know To Be A Successful Online College Student

Diane Hamilton, Ph.D.

ISBN: 0982742800
ISBN-13: 9780982742808
LCCN: 2010905665

DEDICATION

For my mother, who actually taught me how to read when I was only two years old. Thank you for instilling a lifelong desire for education in me. I love you, as well as my husband Bob, daughters Terra and Toni, and the rest of my family...thanks to all of you for your support.

Table of Contents

INTRODUCTION

If you are new to the online education experience, my guess is that you are a bit nervous or apprehensive. It is only natural to feel this way, because this is a very different way of learning for many people, however online college courses are becoming a much more popular form of education. Not only are classes delivered differently, but the average student is also different. Online learners are a very diverse group. Those attending online colleges may have graduated high school last week, 30 years ago, or even long before that. Many online learners may have typed their last term paper on a typewriter, and may not have had much experience using a computer. Suddenly they are online, utilizing fancy software and learning complicated formatting guidelines, and many are unsure of themselves.

What is Unique About This Book

I wrote this book to be used as a tool for those who want to take online courses but feel they could use some guidance about how to be successful. Many colleges that offer online courses offer an initial "how to" course that is helpful for students. In fact, I have taught similar courses many times, and a lot of the things I will be writing about here come from my experience teaching those courses. I believe that students who have a book like this one to read before even beginning an introductory course will have a much easier time understanding how to find things, how to participate, and what all the buzz words mean. This will give them a much greater chance of success, and a lot less frustration.

My research indicates that there are not a lot of helpful books available out there for the prospective online learner. The books I found focused more on explaining which schools were out there, presented technical information in examples that would likely be overwhelming to new students, or just did not cover some of the basics about what to expect online, or provide definitions of important terminology. For example, I think it is important to know how to find the proper school, get loan information, etc., however many of the books on the subject of online learning forget to include some of the most important answers to the questions that I find most online students asking. I have even found myself posting a lot of helpful tips in class for my master-level students, because over the years many professors have failed to help these students understand some of the basic things they need in order to have a strong foundation. This book is meant to be a helpful "go to" resource where you can find answers to the things that most online students usually have to discover through trial and error. Armed with this information, you may just avoid a loss of credit or grade points and start out ahead of the class!

Finding the Information You Need

I have divided the book up into chapters that make it easy for you to look up things that you will run into in your classroom sooner or later, while the glossary at the back has helpful explanations of commonly used terms. There is also an extremely useful Appendices section that has numerous lists and forms that I refer to frequently. The Glossary and Appendices are two of the most important areas of this book, because they summarize all of the key words and examples that you will likely go to for help in easy-to-understand lists and charts. My recommendation for the potential online learner is to read the book in its entirety first, and then once classes begin, you can go back later and find help in the areas where you run into issues, however just reading the Glossary and Appendices in this book will give you more useful information than you will find in any other online student book I have seen on the market.

What I've Gained Through Experience

What makes me qualified to give this advice? Not only have I taken many online courses, but I have also completed an online degree, so I understand things from the student's perspective. Where I have learned the most about what the new online learner requires, however, has been the many years I have spent teaching a large number of online college courses. These courses have included everything from the very first online course that students take in order to learn to be an online student, all the way through to higher-level bachelor's, master's and doctoral courses. In short, I have taught thousands of online learners. During this time, I have found that many colleges use different software (or platforms) in order to deliver their courses. Because I have taught at many different universities, I have experience in the most widely used platforms out there. I have designed courses, written curriculums (course content), and participated in just about every possible type of online format, including utilizing YouTube and Wikis. I imagine that many of you are familiar with YouTube, the online site where you can access videos that have been uploaded, but for those of you who are unfamiliar with a Wiki, it is a Web site that allows multiple users to change the content on that site. A Wiki can also be used as a form of a classroom. One very popular Wiki is called Wikipedia. To see what that looks like, you can go to www.wikipedia.com, but for now, my point is that I have taught in just about every online format available.

Because I have had an extensive amount of online teaching experience, I have seen a lot of worried first-time students. A lot! I feel badly for them, because so many of them feel overwhelmed and unprepared. I want to help students who are anxious about online learning – or even fear it – to embrace it and look forward to all that it has to offer. Personally, I love the online learning experience, and want to share that passion. I have received three major degrees in my life. One I completed in a traditional college, another I did through what used to be referred to as distance learning (sometimes called correspondence learning), which consisted primarily of mailing assignments back and forth, and the last one I undertook online. Of my three degrees, I found that online learning was the absolute best way to learn and achieve my goals.

Things to Like About Online Learning

There are some who question how good an education one gets online, and it's a valid question. My personal experience is that I received the best education of all through online learning. That isn't to say that there aren't 'diploma mills' out there that will basically sell you an education that is neither respected nor valid. When I refer to online learning, I am only referring to those colleges that are accredited, or working towards receiving accreditation. I will explain accreditation a little later, but for now, suffice it to say that regionally accredited online universities deliver some of the best education available.

There is a lot to like about online learning. Many courses are asynchronous, which means you can do your learning and be online at any time during the day (or night, for that matter) rather than at a specific time. This is wonderful for someone like me who does their best work at 5 am! For those people with busy work schedules, kids to raise, or families they want to spend time with, having the flexibility to do their school work at odd hours can be a huge benefit. For those who are shy and prefer not to have people judge them if they ask a question, the privacy of online learning is also a big plus! Online students enjoy the ability to have their questions delivered directly to the professor, and only the professor, should they prefer it that way.

What Type of Person Takes Online Courses

What kind of personality is drawn to online learning? The diversity of students is one of the best parts of being online. Having studied and written a book about personalities and personality assessments (see my Web site at www.drdianehamilton.com), I have done a lot of research about introverts and extroverts. There are numerous definitions for these terms, but for our purposes, a simple definition of an introvert is a person who prefers to think internally, and take their time to come up with an answer. A simple definition of an extrovert is a person who thinks out loud, and may blurt out what they are thinking rather than taking the time to process it internally. I have found that a lot of introverts really enjoy the online atmosphere, because if a question is asked, they are not put on the spot and forced to spit out an answer immediately. They can take the time to consider the question, form their opinion, and think about what they want to say. In a face-to-face classroom situation, this is generally not possible. For the extrovert, who may sometimes wish later that they hadn't just blurted out the first thought that came into their head, the time delay can also be beneficial.

No matter what your age, educational experience or background, this book will help you learn the basics about what it takes to be successful in the online environment. You will learn the buzz words and discover the importance of academic honesty, goal setting, time management and organizational skills. You will find out about the software you will be using, and how to set up your papers so that you wow your professors! You will learn how to gain better comprehension from your study efforts, and improve your test-taking abilities. You will have access to easy-to-understand checklists and helpful examples of online tools that will put you way ahead of your fellow students once class begins. In the end, you will see how all of this can help you plan for a better future. Online learning is the future, and I commend you for taking the first step toward improving your life through receiving a higher education.

CHAPTER 1: ONLINE BASICS

"Education is the key to unlock the golden door of freedom."
~George Washington Carver

Congratulations! You've decided to get an online degree, or what some people refer to as a distance learning degree. This is a big decision, and one that will reap great rewards later. Now that you have made that commitment to yourself, it's time to decide which college you should attend and what degree best fits your needs. That sounds simple, doesn't it? Well, you might be surprised at how many schools and degrees there are to choose from out there. Not only are the strictly online colleges offering distance education, but the traditional brick-and-mortar colleges are as well. "In the 2006–07 academic year, 66 percent of the 4,160 2-year and 4-year Title IV degree-granting postsecondary institutions in the nation offered college-level distance education courses. The overall percentage includes 97 percent of public 2-year institutions, 18 percent of private for-profit 2-year institutions, 89 percent of public 4-year institutions, 53 percent of private not-for-profit institutions, and

70 percent of private for-profit 4-year institutions." (nces. ed.gov, 2010). In the last few years, the numbers have continued to grow due to the increasing popularity of online learning.

Accreditation

How do you choose the right school for you? The first thing you need to be familiar with is the term "accreditation". You will need to find out if the school you are considering is accredited. What is accreditation? "Quite simply, it is a validation – a statement by a group of persons who are, theoretically, impartial experts in higher education – that a given school, or department within a school, has been thoroughly investigated and found worthy of approval" (Bear & Nixon, 2006, p. 37). "There are no accreditation agencies designed specifically for online colleges, and online schools must be accredited in the same way as traditional colleges. This means that your degree from a regionally accredited online college will be just as valuable as one from a brick-and-mortar institution, and as widely accepted as one as well." (AccreditedOnlineColleges.com, 2010). Not only are schools accredited (institutional accreditation), but their individual programs (specialized accreditation) may be as well. There are six regional accrediting organizations that can grant this accreditation in the U.S.:

Middle States Association of Colleges and Schools
www.msche.org.
New England Association of Schools and Colleges
www.ctci.neasc.org.
Northwest Commission on Colleges and Universities
www.nwccu.org.
Northcentral Association of Colleges and Schools
http://www.ncacasi.org.
Southern Association of Colleges and Schools
www.sacscoc.org.
Western Association of Schools and Colleges
www.accjc.org.

Why is it important to find out if the school you are considering is properly accredited? For one thing, you want to be sure you are getting the highest-quality education possible. "If you are planning on transferring to another school at any point, you should know that regionally accredited institutions generally do not accept credits from nationally accredited schools. However, nationally accredited schools will almost always accept credit from both regionally or nationally accredited institutions." (AccreditedOnlineColleges.com, 2010). You also want to be sure that after you have spent a lot of time, money and effort getting your degree, employers will recognize that as a quality education. You also want to be careful that you are not getting a degree from what many have referred to as a "diploma mill".

Diploma Mills

A diploma mill is a school that is more concerned about simply making money from you, and just giving out diplomas for that money, than the education you receive. "A diploma mill or degree mill will pose as a real university and rewards degrees without any evaluation or very little academic work from its students. They make money by selling printed degrees and providing academic references and falsified transcripts to individuals who purchase degrees from them" (elearners.com, 2010). Technically, you can buy just about anything out there, but what good is a piece of paper that says you have a degree when you didn't learn anything, or do anything to get it other than pay money? That is why it is very important to check out the school's accreditation before you pay for anything, to be sure you are getting a quality education that will be well-respected and worthwhile. Be wary of accreditation claims: "On its Web site, Columbus University claims that it is the established name in distance education and also claims that it is accredited by the Adult Higher Education Alliance. This is a fake accrediting agency" (elearners.com, 2010). I would also suggest checking out http://www.elearners.com/resources/agencies.asp to see a list of accrediting agencies.

How can you be sure the school you are interested in is reputable? Quite simply, you need to do some research. According to eLearners.com, you can do the following if you have any doubts about an online program: "See if the online school is accredited, and by whom. Check to see if the accrediting agency is officially sanctioned. Lists are available from several accrediting organizations. Check with the licensing boards and professional associations to see if the program delivers an acceptable level of training. Don't limit your research to classified ads or surveying the Web in search of the right course or program. Call or write the Better Business Bureau and the attorney general's office to make sure the school is operating legally in a state and to see if anyone has filed a complaint. Find out if the school is connected to an established, reputable parent company. If you intend to transfer any online credits earned to another college or university, early on check with that institution to see if they will accept those credits. Ask about the faculty" (eLearners.com, 2010).

Popularity of Online Learning

How popular is online learning? According to the Sloan Consortium "Over 4.6 million students were taking at least one online course during the fall of 2008 term; a 17 percent increase over the number reported the previous year. The 17 percent growth rate for online enrollments far exceeds the 1.2 percent growth of the overall higher education student population." (Sloan, 2010, p. 1). With the growth of the Internet, the ease of accessibility to computers and the flexibility that the online environment affords students, online learning has become more popular than ever. The advantages of not having to buy gas to get to class, not having find a car park or pay for parking, and being able to attend class at any time of the day or night have all contributed to its popularity.

A large percentage of students who are studying on-line are working on their associates, but there are bac-calaureate, master, and doctoral programs available online as well. Much of the growth that has occurred in online learning has happened since 1999. With the re-cent changes in the economy, online classes have seen a surge in enrollment. "Bad economic times have often been good for education, either because decreased availability of good jobs encourages more people to seek education instead, or because those currently em-ployed seek to improve their chances for advancement by pursuing their education" (Sloan, 2008, p. 9).

Competition by Online Institutions

Because online learning is becoming so popular, schools are facing increased competition for students, and so are offering an ever-broader range of courses and degrees in order to appeal to an increasingly diverse group of potential students. According to a profile of undergraduates in the U.S. Postsecondary Education Institutions by the National Center for Education Statistics, online programs are being offered in the following areas of study:

Business
Liberal arts and sciences, general studies, humanities
Health professions and related sciences
Education
Computer and information sciences
Social sciences and history
Psychology
Engineering (Sloan, 2008, p. 12).

With so many options for online learning out there, what is the latest perception of the quality of the experience? In the past, online learning was sometimes looked down on by those who believed that face-to-face instruction was the only way to go. This outlook has changed recently. When looking at perceptions of low quality in online learning, "When asked to compare learning outcomes in online courses with those for face-to-face instruction, academic leaders put the two on very close terms, and expected the online offerings to continue to get better relative to face-to-face options"

(Sloan, 2004, p. 14). In fact, "A recent survey conducted by a company called Zogby International found that 83 percent of executives rated online degrees as credible as those earned in a traditional on-campus setting" (elearners.com, 2010).

Employer and Military Help

Now that there are so many online choices, how does this affect the cost for the students? Many schools provide grants, and student loans can always be obtained. As with any other school, there may also be merit scholarships available. Many employers are also willing to pay for their employees to improve their education. According to eLearners.com (2006), "IRS regulations stipulate that employers may provide an employee with up to $5,250 per year, tax-free" (eLearners, 2006, p. 7). Many employers often stipulate that students must receive a certain grade in order to receive the funds, so be sure to check their requirements. The military also provides assistance with education. The Web sites to check for each branch of the service are:

Army:
http://www.soc.aascu.org/socad/Default.html
Army National Guard:
http://www.soc.aascu.org/socguard/Default.html

Coast Guard:
http://www.soc.aascu.org/soccoast/Default.html
Navy:
http://ww.soc.aascu.org/socnav/Default.html
Marines:
http://www.soc.aascu.org/socmar/Default.html

Choosing the Right Classes for You

Once you decide that you are ready to get an online education, you must consider the types of colleges that are available to you. There are two-year and four-year colleges and universities, both private and public, and some are for profit and some are not for profit. Each has their own advantages and disadvantages. Things to consider when choosing your school include costs, majors offered, reputation of the school, how often courses are offered, length of each course, flexibility, and, of course, accreditation. An important consideration is the length of the courses offered. Are you the type who does well when the course is short and right to the point? If so, you might want to look for a college that offers five- or six-week courses. Are you the type who doesn't like to be rushed through a course? Then you might want to look at the eight-, nine- or even 15-week courses. Most schools have a certain way in which they offer their classes. For example, they usually have all of their bachelor's courses the same length, i.e., if one is six weeks, they're probably all six weeks.

How do you know if you are a good candidate for online learning? I feel like Jeff Foxworthy here, but you may be a good candidate for being an online learner if you:

Have an unusual work or family schedule
Need to travel a lot
Are self-motivated
Like the thought of accelerated learning
Want to meet a diverse group of people
Like technology
Hate driving and parking and walking to class
Have a physical disability
Are independent
Live in another country
Love chat rooms and typing
Love learning in all formats

Many careers sites such as Careerbuilder.com have useful articles for students thinking about getting an online degree. "Tips for finding a quality online degree: Are you interested in going to back to school online? Here are six things to consider when looking for a quality online-degree program:

1. Reputation – Is it an institution that provides only online degrees, or does it have physical locations as well? Having actual campuses helps to establish credibility. A red flag would be the existence of only a post office box or suite number.

2. Accreditation – The Department of Education says that researching the accreditation is essential. Diploma mills are usually accredited by fake agencies. It's important to make sure the accrediting agency is one recognized by the Department or the Council for Higher Education Accreditation.

3. Accessibility – Does the school offer technical help and easy access to advisers, professors and the help desk?

4. How quickly can you earn the degree? – A red flag would be earning a bachelor's degree in just months.

5. Program fees – Students should pay as they go and be charged per credit hour, rather than per program.

6. How hard is the work? – Diploma mills require very little work and often take life or work experience

into account. Legitimate programs require the same amount of work one would expect attending class on a campus" (Careerbuilder.com, 2010).

Paying for Online Learning

Just because you want to go back to school doesn't necessarily mean you have the money sitting around to pay for it. Many students are looking for ways to finance their education, and options include student loans, company reimbursement, grants and scholarships. There are some job areas where they need people so badly that there may be opportunities where the government forgives your loan. Some of the areas where there are currently shortages include nursing, teaching, law and the military. For more information on loan forgiveness, check out the following web site: http://www.opm.gov/oca/pay/studentloan/html/fy05report.pdf. For public service loan forgiveness programs,
check out: http://www.finaid.org/loans/publicservice.phtml.

Some fields allow volunteering your time to count toward loan relief. For example, check out the AmeriCorps at http://www.americorps.org, the Peace Corps at http://www.peacecorps.gov and Volunteers in Service to American (VISTA) at: http://www.friendsofvista.org.

Student loan areas to check out include the Stafford loan program. "Stafford loans are federal student loans made available to college and university students to supplement personal and family resources, scholarships, grants, and work-study. Nearly all students are eligible to receive Stafford loans regardless of credit. Stafford loans may be subsidized by the U.S. Government or unsubsidized depending on the student's need." (Staffordloan.com, 2010).

Another program is the Pell Grant. "The Federal Pell Grant program is a federal aid program that provides financial assistance to students otherwise unable to afford an undergraduate education. Your school can either credit the Pell Grant funds to your school account, pay you directly (usually by check), or combine these methods. The school must tell you in writing how and when you'll be paid, and how much your award will be. Schools must pay you at least once per term (semester, trimester, or quarter). Schools that do not use formally defined, traditional terms must pay you at least twice per academic year" (college-scholarships-grants.biz, 2010).

There are other ways to help pay for your online education on your own. According to eLearners.com (2010) you should speak to your financial advisor about the possibility of using:

1. Personal savings
2. Credit cards
3. Funds borrowed from your 401k or Retirement Plan
4. Funds borrowed against a life insurance policy
5. A line of credit or HELOC (home equity line of credit)
6. A family loan or gift
7. Loans from the traditional lending agencies such as Sallie Mae at http://www.tuitionpay.com/ or Tuition Management Systems at http://www.afford.com or FACTS Management Company at http://www.factsmgt.com/FACTS/Family.

The most important first step is to talk to your school's financial advisors to find out what options are available to you. For more information about completing the application for federal student financial aid, be sure to check out http://www.fafsa.ed.gov/. If you are not familiar with FASFA, "Today, Federal Student Aid performs a range of critical functions that include, among others:

- Educating students and families on the process of obtaining aid;
- Processing millions of student financial aid applications each year;
- Disbursing billions of dollars in aid funds to students through schools;
- Enforcing financial aid rules and regulations;

- Servicing millions of student loan accounts, and securing repayment from borrowers who have defaulted on their loans; and
- Operating information technology systems and tools that manage billions in student aid dollars" (federalstudentaid.ed.gov, 2010).

Do not get discouraged, because there are many loans and finance programs out there. "During the 2006–07 academic year, more than $130 billion in financial aid was distributed to undergraduate and graduate students in the form of grants from all sources and federal loans, work-study, and tax credits and deductions. In addition, these students borrowed more than $18 billion from state and private sources to help finance their education" (collegeboard.com, 2010). I recommend that you download the most recent Trends in Student Aid report from http://www.collegeboard.com/prod_downloads/about/news_info/trends/trends_aid_07.pdf.

Recent Government Changes to Lending Programs

There were some big changes to the government school loan programs in 2009. Remember, should you be able to qualify for a loan, check with your tax preparer to find out about the interest you can deduct from your taxes. For the latest information on the American

Opportunity Credit, the Hope Credit, and the Lifetime Learning Credit, as well as savings plans, deductions and scholarship information, check out the following web site: http://www.irs.gov/newsroom/article/0,,id=213044,00.html.

To be sure you are getting the right amount of financial aid, U.S. News and World Report recently suggested that you ask your college financial advisor the following 10 questions:

1. The college's policy on student loans
2. The way the college calculates a family's need
3. What the college considers as its cost
4. The college's expectation for a student contribution
5. How the college counts home equity
6. How the college considers divorced parents
7. The cutoff date for the meet-full-needs promise
8. The aid policy for international students
9. Whether the school also offers merit scholarships
10. The effect of an aid application on chances for admission" (usnews.com, 2010).

Questions about Classmates

Once you find the funds to pay for school, that's when a lot of the questions about how it all works begin. You may wonder who your fellow online classmates will be. That is the beauty of online learning. The diversity of the students allows for interesting discussions and learn-ing opportunities in class. "Adult learners are likely to be married and have children—especially if they are age 30 or older. The exception is low-income adult students who are more likely to be single parents" (eLearners, 2006, p. 46). Many classes are made up of students from all over the country, and sometimes from around the world, and a lot of classes facilitate asynchronous communi-cation. This means that there is no specific time when students have to be online, therefore people from all around the world can sign on at any time of the day.

How Tech-Savvy Do I Need to Be?

Because it is all online, does that mean that you have to be a computer guru? No, you don't have to be a guru, but you do need to have some basic skills. For example, it helps if you know how to type, but even if you can only 'hunt and peck,' that will work – it may just take you a little longer to type your papers. Usually, students should have the ability to use Microsoft Word to type their papers, and to upload a file as an attach-ment. Most schools offer an introductory class that gets you comfortable with online classes and how they work, and also have a technical support number to call if you can't figure out how to upload a file, or if something just doesn't seem to be working correctly. Usually, students who feel comfortable enough to enroll in an online class find that they are getting on pretty well by the second week of class.

Help With the Basics

It's a good idea if the new online learner can find a mentor to help them with the basics. Many students know someone who has undertaken online classes before, and can answer basic questions. A mentor is a good resource to have at the outset, when you are feeling unsure. Also remember that the professor is there to answer your questions, so don't hesitate to contact them. Many schools require that their professors provide answers to your questions within 24 hours. For students who are shy about asking questions, the online environment allows them to ask questions without embarrassment.

If you have questions that are specific to technology issues, you will likely need to contact the school's technical support staff. I recommend that you write down contact numbers for your professor, your counselor and your school's technical support line on the form that is included in the Appendix at the back of this book.

There are several issues you may have where the technical support staff can assist you:

- Inability to access the class, or online materials for the class
- Inability to upload assignments and attach files
- Unexplained error messages
- Password changes or being locked out
- An online test that shuts you out before you have completed it.

However, there are several issues you may have where technical support staff cannot assist you:

- Your computer crashes
- Your Internet service provider isn't responding
- You have contracted a virus
- You did not back up your files.

If you do find that you have to contact technical support, be sure that they give you proof that you have had them working on your problems. Usually, they will assign you a case number that you can use to show your professor that you experienced issues that were beyond your control. Always include a description of the technical support issue, together with the ticket number, when you upload your assignment.

CHAPTER 2: NAVIGATING ONLINE

"I think it's fair to say that personal computers have become the most empowering tool we've ever created. They're tools of communication, they're tools of creativity, and they can be shaped by their user."
~Bill Gates

Many students can be intimidated by what they perceive as the complexities of online learning, and many new online students state that they are confused by some of the online jargon as well. I find, however, that many of my students who are initially overwhelmed find that in less than a couple of weeks, they feel much more comfortable. If an online student learns some of the terminology that online courses use before starting their first class, it will make their experience much less frustrating. Not all online schools use exactly the same terminology. However, based on my experience working for many different online universities, there are several terms that are used by most of them. This chapter discusses terms you should become familiar with, many of which can also be found in the glossary at the back of the book.

What kind of Computer Setup Do I Need?

Technology can also be intimidating to many people who have not done much more than emailing or some light Web surfing. The hardware and software requirements are something that your guidance counselor can give you more information about before you start. However, most students should at least have a fairly up-to-date computer with a reliable Internet connection. You should also have working speakers on your computer for those assignments that requirement you to listen to audio files. You will probably need to have word-processing software that enables files to be saved in ".doc" or ".docx" format, and some classes may require PowerPoint software as well. Microsoft has a student edition of their Office software package that has all the key software, such as Word and PowerPoint, that you will need for your personal computer (PC) or Apple computer (Mac). Check around for some price breaks. I have seen Office offered at discounted prices on sites like Amazon. Lastly, be sure you have good virus protection software, like Norton Antivirus or McAfee Antivirus. For more information about Norton, check out www.norton.com or for McAfee check out www.mcafee.com. I use Norton, which I can recommend.

The University of Phoenix, which has the largest number of online students in North America, lists the following as their minimum hardware and software requirements. Note that these requirements will change as technology changes, and so you may need to update from time to time as needed.

Basic Requirements:

- A processor of 1.6 GHz or faster
- A current anti-virus application—updated regularly
- 256MB RAM or greater
- 20 GB hard drive or larger
- 56.6 kbps modem or high-speed Internet connection
- Monitor and video card with 1024x768 ppi or greater resolution
- Sound card with speakers
- CD ROM
- Inkjet or laser printer
- Email address
- Internet service provider (ISP) account
- Microsoft® Internet Explorer® version 6.0 or later
- Adobe® Reader® 6.0 or later
- Microsoft® Outlook Express 6.0 or later
- Microsoft® Office XP, 2003, 2004 or 2007
- Microsoft® Word
- Microsoft® PowerPoint®
- Flash® Player (www.phoenix.edu, 2010).

Don't Forget to Backup!

This list may seem overwhelming to someone who has minimal computer knowledge, however, with the newer computers that are out there today, these requirements are not difficult to accommodate. In fact, many items may come as standard with the computer you have purchased, or can easily be added. The only thing I would add to that list is some form of backup, such as a flash drive. It is extremely important to back up all of your work on a flash drive so that not only will you have a copy of that important paper if your computer crashes, but your work is also in a portable format, so that should you need to use another computer, it's easy to transfer your work.

Terminology

Even if you're familiar with computers and software, there will still be some terminology that may have a different meaning in the context of online education. One of the most frequent terms a student will hear is the word 'classroom'. Sounds like a pretty basic word, right? Well... maybe. What may be confusing is that instead of having one area or classroom where a student finds everything they need for their course, they may actually have to locate several areas. Usually, there is a main Web page for the learning institution where a student logs in. Once they are logged in to the university, they then click on a link that gets them into their classroom. However, this is where the fun begins. Once they have entered the main classroom, there may be various areas the need to locate within that software. Depending upon the platform (which is the fancy word for software program) that the school uses, there may be several areas where students will post things and find things.

What is a Platform?

Many schools use software platforms such as Blackboard, eCollege, and OLS to deliver their classes. I will give examples using these three programs in this chapter, since these are the most frequently utilized platforms. Don't worry, though – I won't spend time giving examples of software you have not yet seen, because that would defeat the purpose of this book, which is to be a simple user's manual. However, I feel it is important to include some mention of these software packages to better explain some of the terminology that is commonly used. I would recommend coming back to this section later after you have actually started your course, when the references will make more sense, depending on the type of software your school uses.

How Classes are Taught

Within most classes, there is usually a main classroom, and a discussion board or discussion area, a forum where students interact and participate in weekly discussions based on what has been taught. Most often, this is not the area where students will post homework. In the software program called Blackboard, this area is called the Discussion Board. In eCollege, there is usually a tab set up on the left under the appropriate week labeled 'Discussion'. In OLS, the area may be called 'Discussion' or 'Main Forum'. The most confusing thing for students is that they often expect everything to occur in one main area, but often, that is not the case. This main area must be thought of solely as the discussion room, and not as an area where homework is actually posted.

There may also be an area that is called the "chat room". Many schools have a link to an area where students can just talk about class, or more personal things, just as if they were hanging out in the hallway in a regular school. Some students just post messages about how things are going for them. Many of my technology students like to post information about cool games they have been playing. Depending on the school and the level of the course, the chat room may get a lot of chat or it may get very little. Sometimes, students don't realize that they have this opportunity to socialize and to share problems and concerns. I recommend posting things occasionally to try and develop friendships with your fellow students. As an online student, you may end up taking several classes with many of the same students, so the chat room is a good meeting ground, a place where you can get to know people you may come across in future courses. It is not an area where you post homework, or where anything you post will receive credit. It is not a place to ask questions important questions, either, because the professor may not regularly monitor it.

There is usually another area where students will post their actual assignments and ask questions of the professor in private. Right now, before class begins, this information may not make sense, because you haven't seen the software yet, however once you get into class, I recommend coming back to this section to remind yourself how to find this area. In Blackboard, there are usually weekly assignments set up on the tabs on the left. For week one, a student would look at what was required by going into the tab for week one, which should include a link that can be clicked on to show any homework that needs to be submitted. For eCollege, there is something called a dropbox. When students click on the dropbox, there is usually a link whereby they can upload their homework. For OLS, students usually post their assignments in their individual classroom. Okay, that's it for individual software references. I don't want you to get bogged down worrying about the complexities of the software, because it will be much clearer when you're actually looking at it online. It is, however, important to provide this information for those of you who go online when class starts and can't remember where to go.

All schools have different requirements regarding how and when classes will be held. If a class is asynchronous, that means that you can log on at any time, day or night. If the class is synchronous, that means there is a specific time when everyone must log on. Every school has a different way of accessing materials for courses, too. Many schools are starting to offer online textbooks, which means you can access the text from any computer, and download the information you need. Some schools have team activities, while others have strictly individual assignments. Some schools require professors to deliver audio or video lectures, while others allow typed-up lectures, and still others may not require lectures at all.

Attendance vs. Participation

Many schools have requirements about attendance and participation, and I'm warning you right now, this is one area where many first-time online students have difficulty understanding the difference between these two words. What students need to realize is that these two terms do not mean the same thing. Attendance is more about showing up, and posting just about anything. It means you entered the class, and posted something somewhere. You might have just said hello to someone in a chat room, or you may have uploaded an assignment or contributed to a discussion. Whatever it was that you posted, the school's software showed that you took the time to post something, which means you were in attendance that day. Most schools like to see that students are showing up to class, or being in attendance, at least a couple of times a week, if not more.

However, this is not to be confused with participation. Participation is more about actually posting something of relevance in a current discussion. Many schools require students to respond to discussion questions every week, and their responses to these discussion questions count as participation. Posting in a chat room is not participation, but if you respond to a discussion question posted by the professor in the main classroom, preferably in a thoughtful way, even if you don't fully understand the topic yet – that would be participation. Keep in mind that there are usually guidelines as to what qualifies as a participation post that is deemed worthy of credit. Many schools require that your post or response be substantive. That means it has to have some depth to it. The professor usually posts guidelines as to what constitutes a good posting. For example, they might say that a posting needs to be at least 150 words. Don't expect to get credit for posting a response that is just basically agreeing with what someone else said, though, even if you manage to take 150 words to do it. Students who simply post something like "I agree" or "You are right" or similarly brief answers probably won't receive participation credit, nor will students who post responses that are basically random thought bubbles, no matter how long they are, unless they happen to be studying creative writing, in which case they might just get away with it.

Discussions and Interactions

If you've never attended an online class, you may have several questions about what you expect to find in your classroom. To start with, you will be interacting with the professor of the course, as well as your fellow classmates. Some classes I have taught have had as few as five students, while others have had as many as 30, but you should expect around 10 to 20 students to be available to interact with in your typical course.

This interacting is usually done by way of a discussion. You may be wondering – how does one post to a discussion? Posting to discussions is not all that different from responding to blogs or emails or tweets; you read the last post (and preferably those before it to put things into context), hit reply, and post your answer. Usually, a new question is posted by the instructor as a new thread. A thread is a term that basically means a topic. It is called a thread because as people continue to respond to the initial posting, they create a long list of postings, all hanging off the initial question – like a thread. Some schools require students to start a new discussion or thread every time they post, while other schools want you to reply to the question that an instructor has posted. It is important to read the professor's instructions, to ensure that you are either creating or responding to threads in the preferred manner.

Discussions are usually held in the main classroom, and may occur every week. Think of this as you would a regular classroom, where the teacher asks a question, and the students attempt to answer that question. What is different about online learning is that you have time to formulate your answers, whereas in a face-to-face setting, you are often put on the spot. This is one of the big advantages of online learning. I have found that students who are more introverted really prefer the additional time they get to respond. To learn more out about personality issues, see Chapter 8 about specific personality types and the online environment.

<u>Grading</u>

Having spent the week discussing the topic and posting your homework, you will find that there are different ways in which you might view your grades. Most schools have the professors post a syllabus on the first day of class that gives provides all the important information you need to know in relation to that course. You should look for the syllabus before you do anything else, and print it out. The syllabus usually tells you what the requirements are for the course, and how the grading scale will be applied. There is an example of a course syllabus in the Appendix at the back of the book.

In terms of finding your grades, each software program has a different method of delivery. If you are using Blackboard, I have seen some schools deliver grades in an area that lists all the grades together. I have also schools create a tab on the left called "Feedback", where students can also receive a weekly update from the instructor on the specifics of how they did that week. If you are using eCollege, the papers that you left in the dropbox will be returned in the same way they were dropped off, but will now include a grade and teacher comments. If you are using OLS, you will get a posting in your individual classroom showing your grade, along with comments from the professor.

The Syllabus and the Calendar

Some professors will post both a syllabus and a calendar. Sometimes, the due dates for assignments are listed on the calendar, and sometimes they are listed on the syllabus. The Appendix at the back of this book includes examples of a very basic calendar, as well as a very basic syllabus, but for now I have included a simple example of a calendar and a syllabus below, where 'X's have been substituted for the actual course information that would normally be included. The most important thing you can do when you first find these items in your classroom is to be sure to print them off and put them in a place where you will be able to see them clearly.

	M	Tu	W	Th	F	S	Su
	Day 1	Day 2	Day 3	Day 4	Day 5	Day 6	Day 7
Week 1							
	Post Bio		Assignment Due				Paper Due
	Remember to post at least X number of postings over X days during the week						
Week 2							
			Assignment Due				Paper Due
	Remember to post at least X number of postings over X days during the week						
Week 3							
			Assignment Due				Midterm Exam
	Remember to post at least X number of postings over X days during the week						
Week 4							
			Assignment Due				Paper Due
	Remember to post at least X number of postings over X days during the week						
Week 5							
			Assignment Due				Final Exam
	Remember to post at least X number of postings over X days during the week						

Sample Calendar

Prerequisites	There are no prerequisites for this course.
Teacher's Information	Teacher's bio may be posted here.
Course Description	This course will introduce students to XXXX concepts about the subject. Students will explore XXXX aspects about the subject. Some schools will list all assignments due here as well.
Course Objectives Or Outcomes	• Student will participate in discussions. • Student will write X number of expository essays on topics related to this course. • Student will be able to explain X topic. • Student will be able to compare and contrast X and X items. • Student will be able to distinguish between X and X.
Course Policies and Procedures	**Grading Criteria** Overall assessment for this course may be based on writings, discussion questions, essays, and quizzes.

50	Papers/ Assignments
30	Discussion Online
20	Final

Grading Scale
The grading scale for this class is pretty standard and straightforward:

A	90-100
B	80-89
C	70-79
D	60-69
F	Below 60

Late papers: Assignments will be marked 10% off for each day that they are late, up to a maximum of 4 days late. The final cannot be turned in after due date.

Plagiarism consists of using another author's words without proper identification and documentation. It is unacceptable.

Textbook[s]   Required: Text and Author

Sample Syllabus

You will note that there is usually a grade scale listed on the syllabus, but there's no universal grade scale that all schools use. I have seen a lot of schools that use the traditional 90–100% is an A, 80–89% is a B, 70–79 is a C, 60–69 is a D, and anything below 60 is an F, however it is not unusual for master level and higher courses to only have A, B, C, and F. Further, it is not unusual for schools to have the scales include A–, B+, and so on. It is important that you make note of what qualifies as a passing score. Some schools require a C to pass, while others may allow a D to pass. If your employer is paying for your schooling, be sure to find out what their requirements are for reimbursement. They may require a B or higher in order for you to receive payment.

What is a Rubric?

It is also important for the first time online student to be aware of something called a "rubric". A rubric is just a fancy word for a chart, or an explanation of how many points are assigned for certain things in a paper or on a test. It is very important for students to look at all rubrics that are posted before working on any assignments. I have had many students who continue to make the same mistakes over and over because they do not read the rubric before the assignment, and/or they do not read the comments on their papers, or on the returned

Example Rubric

rubric, after the assignment. For a full-size example of what a rubric looks like, please see the Appendix at the back of the book. In the meantime, here is a smaller version to give you an idea of what they look like.

Although this may seem confusing now, the good news is, once you know what platform your college uses, you can come back and review all of this information to remind you where to look. It is also important to remember that schools usually have you enroll in a very basic introductory online course that teaches you how to get around in their classrooms. These classes are very helpful, and will provide good guidance, just as this book will help you to learn the basics. The advantage you will have by reading this book first is that when you see all of these things in your classroom, they will make a lot more sense, because you will be ahead of the game!

Replying and Uploading Files

For those of you with limited computer knowledge, there will be a few things you will need to learn to do. You will need to know how to reply to postings, how to upload and attach files, and you should have a basic knowledge of how to use Microsoft Word. I will expand on software issues in later chapters, but for now, replying to postings simply means that when you are in a discussion in class, you are able to click on "reply", type your response and then hit "send". The wording may be slightly different in each platform, but that's usually all you need to know in order to reply to postings and participate in discussions. Uploading can be a little more difficult, but if you have ever attached a picture or a file to an email, it's very similar to that process. Basically, you will have a button somewhere on your homework page that says "browse". You click on that, and then select the file you want to attach. When you are done attaching your file and writing your reply, you will usually just hit "send".

The Library and Search Engines

Areas other than the classroom that you will want to become familiar with include the online library. There is usually a link within the school's software, either inside or outside of the main classroom, that you can click on to enter the school's library. Usually, schools have search engines within the library that are not all that different from the search engines you've probably used online. They don't work exactly like a Google or Yahoo search, but they do find things in the library, just like those search engines find things on the Web. Some of the main library search engines you will use include EBSCOhost, Gale PowerSearch, and Proquest. Think of these names just as you would Google, Yahoo, and Bing. Once you get into these programs within the library, they allow you to search for articles and find resources to help you with your papers you will be writing. Most of them have a search line just like Google and the other Web search engines. In addition, these library search engines have some filters that can be very helpful. For example, there may be boxes you can check that say things like "peer reviewed scholarly journals". If you click on that box, the search will only bring up articles that have been peer reviewed and are published in scholarly journals. The importance of this will become clear later on when you begin to write essays. For now, it is important for you to realize that there are ways to filter the things you search for in the library that will help you narrow down your search.

Interacting with the Professor

Most of your questions about how to use these things can be answered by your professor. At first, many students are apprehensive about asking questions. Sometimes they don't know what to call their teacher/professor. Sometimes they think they are bugging them, and don't want to be seen as annoying. However, they soon realize that the professor is there to help. As for what you should call your professor...that depends. Many professors will tell you in their welcome message what they like to be called, while many sign their name at the end of their postings so you can see what they call themselves. If you see "PhD" after their name, that means they can be called "Dr." If they don't tell you, and you can't see "PhD," it is best to either ask them what they want to be called, or to simply call them "Professor So and So." I usually have my students call me "Dr. Diane," but it would be equally appropriate to call me "Dr. Hamilton" or "Professor Diane" or "Professor Hamilton." It is not appropriate to call your professor by their first name, unless they have told you that it is okay to do so.

Tone and Attitude

Speaking of what is appropriate, this brings to mind something that those of us in online learning refer to as "tone." One of the problems with talking back and forth online is that a person's intended meaning doesn't always come across clearly, so it is important to understand how you are being perceived by others in your class – including the professor. That is what I mean by tone...how your message sounds...how it is perceived. Unfortunately, I see a lot of students communicating in a very negative tone. This can be very upsetting to other students, who do not appreciate being spoken to in this manner. It is very important to always be respectful of others when "speaking" online. Try to avoid sarcasm, which definitely doesn't go down well in the online learning environment. If you think something you've written could be taken two ways, include a smiley face or an explanation to show that your intended meaning is positive. Also, make sure that you check your documents for spelling and punctuation. This reduces the possibility of your fellow classmates and your instructor misconstruing your meaning. It is also important to realize that spell-check does not always catch every problem. Sometimes, when you run spell-check on a document, it will ask you if you mean such and such a word. Be sure that the word you are choosing is the actual word you intended to use. I can't tell you how many times students have written notes to me that said something like, "Please excuse the incontinence." I'm pretty sure they meant to say, "Please excuse the inconvenience."

Formatting

You will find that you end up doing most of your writing using your word processing software, which has spell-check capabilities. Discussion boards usually have this feature as well. I have found in my online teaching experience that the software of choice is Microsoft Word, although I realize that a lot of students use the cheaper "Works" version. The important thing to remember is that most schools require files to be submitted in ".doc" or ".docx" format, which is the default for Microsoft Word. Other software programs use a ".wps" format as their default, which most instructors will not accept. Be sure that when you have finished writing your assignment and go to save it, the file name is something like "Homework1. doc" and not something like "Homework1.wps." If you need help learning how to do this, most schools have technical-support staff on call 24 hours a day to answer these and other computer-related questions.

Who to Know

Along with getting to know technical support people, I would recommend that you get to know your counselor and, of course, your professor, who should be your first point of reference about course content. Don't be afraid to ask questions. They'll soon tell you if they are not the correct person to ask, in which case they will direct you to the correct person. It is also very important that you are well aware of your professor's expectations of you in class. Most professors post this in their syllabus, or elsewhere in the class. Many professors also post a rubric or a spreadsheet for assignments that lists how marks will be assigned. Each professor and each assignment may have different expectations and requirements. If you have any questions, speak up. It will show your professor that you cared enough to ask. Showing interest is always seen as a positive thing.

Mistakes to Avoid

Having taught so many courses over so many years, I have come to see that students tend to keep making the same old mistakes. One of the problems I see is that students often assume that studying online is going to be easier, but I have found the content to be very similar in online and face-to-face courses. While it may be easier in terms of not having to drive, park, pay for gas, take classes at odd hours, etc., it might also require more discipline due to the lack of face-to-face contact.

Another mistake students often make is thinking they can be late in submitting their assignments and still receive full credit. Every professor has a different policy regarding late submission. I usually allow papers to be submitted up to four days late, losing 10% for each day that they are late. Some professors have more lenient guidelines, while others do not accept any late papers at all. The most important thing you can do if you think you are going to be late for a valid reason is to contact the professor beforehand and provide an explanation as to why you will be late. Asking after the fact usually doesn't work out well. You should also understand that having your computer crash is not a valid excuse for being late. Remember, you should be backing up your work, and then there are other ways for you to submit your assignment. You can use the local library, a friend's computer, etc.

Professors have heard every excuse there is. I have never taught a course where I have had students who didn't tell me that someone in their family had died. I truly hope they were lying, because I hate to think that there are so many people out there to whom this is actually happening. However, it has been my experience that the ones who said someone had died had usually been late all along, and had come up with all sorts of other excuses as well. If there have been no other issues, I usually give students the benefit of the doubt. The best thing to do if you have a family member who is ailing is to tell your professor right away, so that in case something does happen, you have alerted them that you have a sensitive situation at hand. If you are late due to a technical problem, be sure you have called technical support and have received a ticket number to show that you were trying to get help. Always include that technical support number with your explanation as to why you were late.

One of the main things I have noticed with online students is that they tend to procrastinate. I have not seen any studies comparing online to face-to-face courses in this regard, however procrastination is something that all students need to work on from the beginning. One way of avoiding it is to have set up a good plan for how you will achieve your goals. This requires setting goals that are measurable, and then planning what needs to be done on a daily basis to achieve them.

While we're discussing things to avoid with online learning, remember, it is never appropriate to plagiarize. We will talk more about this in Chapter 7, but for now, plagiarizing means you have taken someone else's work and claimed it as your own. I once actually had a student who submitted a paper on plagiarism that was plagiarized! How do we know, as professors, that you are plagiarizing? For one thing, we have software programs like TurnItIn that checks your papers to see if it is your work. Often times it can be obvious because the writing style does not match that of previous work. I actually had a student who turned in their final paper still attached to an email that said, "Thank you for purchasing this paper… that will be $15". Yes, you can purchase just about any paper that will ever be required for any class on the Web. The thing is, though, our plagiarism checkers have all of those papers loaded into them, and will easily catch the fact that they are plagiarized. So, save your $15 and write it yourself. Trust me – if you do not, you *will* get caught.

What happens if you get caught plagiarizing? Each school has their own guidelines for how they handle this. Usually your professor starts the ball rolling by letting you know that your work has been found to be plagiarized. They will then notify the university of this fact. The university personnel who handle the hearings will contact you to let you present your case. Penalties range from getting a zero on the paper to being expelled from the institution.

Online learning is not that different from traditional learning when it comes to lack of tolerance for cheat-ing and improper behavior. However, there are many misconceptions about online learning concerning how it differs from traditional education. In the past, there were rumors that perhaps the quality of education was not as good as regular face-to-face learning. A report by SRI International for the Department of Education concluded, "On average, students in online learning conditions performed better than those receiving face-to-face instruction" (U.S. Department of Education, 2009). Personally, I think that online learning is just like face-to-face learning in that some courses (for me, it was statistics) are hard, no matter how you take them, while others (for me, English) are relatively easy no matter how you take them. There is the requirement of having to be computer literate to some extent, however even students taking face-to-face classes will probably need to have some basic computer knowledge in order to type up their papers. Not much more computer literacy is required for online learning. It is also important to note that online learning is much more than just submitting assignments. The perception that students are simply left to work on their own then just email their assignments in is not accurate; I have actually found much more interaction and involvement in my online courses than I had in my face-to-face courses.

Misconceptions about Costs

Lastly, I have heard some people say that online learning is more expensive, while I have also heard others say that it is less expensive than traditional university education. In reality, some online degree programs can cost as much as traditional programs, however there are many that are very affordable, and will cost a student far less on average, more like the cost of attending a community college. For example, the total cost of the MBA program at Kaplan University is $20,540. Listed below are the 2008–2009 College Board statistics for the estimated annual cost of higher education at various institutions.

Community College – $4,552*
In State University – $17,336
Private University – $35,374
*doesn't include room and board (fldcu.org, 2010)

The total cost of the degree for either online or traditional study should include all aspects, including gas to get there, room and board if living there, as well as multiple other factors. "The total tuition you'll pay for an online degree, in fact, may be exactly the same as what you'd pay at a brick-and-mortar college for four years. But you'll get a big financial benefit from the fact that you'll live at home while studying. Students at traditional colleges have to budget tens of thousands of dollars for room and board over four years, especially if their school is in a major city" (successdegrees.com, 2010). It is important to tally the number of courses required, the time required, and all the other factors before deciding whether online study is a cheaper or more expensive investment. For many, including myself, even if online learning came out slightly more expensive, I would still prefer the flexibility and all the other advantages it offers.

CHAPTER 3: ACADEMIC HONESTY

"Borrowed thoughts, like borrowed money,
only show the poverty of the borrower."
~Lady Marquerite Blessington

In the previous chapter I touched briefly on academic honesty and plagiarism, but in some of the classes I teach, I spend many weeks discussing just this one topic. Why is it so important to cover it in such detail? For one thing, it is ethically and morally wrong to steal another person's work. For another, although students often underestimate the importance of turning in their own work, universities take this topic very seriously.

The Importance of Honesty

I often ask students why someone would bother going to class and then just turn in someone else's work. What do you get out of that? Unfortunately, many people forget that the reason they are going to school is to learn. In my opinion, it should be less about the grades and more about what you get out of the learning experience. So many students stress themselves out trying to get a 4.0, or perfect grades. While this is a wonderful thing to strive for, I'm more interested in students acquiring knowledge than achieving good grades. Perhaps because of this, I do not grade too harshly, because I think students are more apt to produce better work if they feel they are going to be rewarded for their efforts.

Plagiarism

However, there are plenty of students who do not put a lot of effort into their work at all, which I find very sad. For those students who are looking to just get a piece of paper and not an education out of the experience, there are plenty of Web sites that offer papers for a fee. As I mentioned in the last chapter, however, all of these papers are in the schools' plagiarism checkers. Sometimes, these software checkers show that the student has merely quoted references incorrectly, and did not actually mean to steal information. It is very important that when the time comes for online students to learn how to cite references, they pay close attention to the rules. Most universities now require papers to be turned in using what is called APA format. "APA" actually stands for American Psychological Association, however APA format is really just a guideline for how the university wants to see papers submitted, with specific margin sizes, indentation requirements, etc. Part of submitting papers in correct APA format includes having any cited work in the correct format as well. Sometimes, a student realizes they are taking someone else's words and intends to show that as a citation, but presents it incorrectly. Plagiarism checkers will pick this up.

If a student is caught plagiarizing, there are several things that could happen. The teacher may see that it is just a mistake, and give a warning, or they may see that it is actual plagiarism and give a zero for the paper or the class and report that student to the school. The school's administrative people will then follow up on the accusation. Students who are caught plagiarizing can fail the course or even be kicked out of school, depending on the severity of the offense.

Citing to Avoid Plagiarism

I have had students ask me what constitutes plagiarism. I wish there was an exact definition of how many words from someone else you can use and still be okay, and how many you can use and not be okay. A good rule of thumb is to not use more than three words in a row from someone else's work without giving them credit. That does not mean you cannot use commonly used expressions like "Once upon a time." However, it is best to write in your own words, and if you need to support something you have said by including a quotation or citation, it will need to be in proper APA format, which you will learn in future English-related courses. For those of you who just can't wait, and want to see an example of what an APA-formatted paper looks like, check out the following link for help: http://my.ilstu.edu/~jhkahn/APAsample.pdf. I would also recommend going to http://owl.english.purdue.edu/owl/resource/560/01/ for some of the specifics that will be required in future courses should papers have an APA requirement, For the time being, however, don't stress too much about APA, because it's not something that will just be dropped on you in your first online course without explanation. For more APA information, check out Chapter 9.

Cutting and Pasting

One very important thing to remember is to never copy and paste information into your papers. Many students make the mistake of thinking they can just go to a Web site and copy a large chunk, if not a whole page, of information and paste it directly into their assignment. This is considered plagiarism. There may be a time when you can copy and paste a particular chart or graph and include the correct citation information about it, however, until you learn how to write in APA format, do not copy and paste anything into your work. You can include the Web site link and say something like, "For more information, you can check out such and such a link." But, be very careful about using copy and paste!

CHAPTER 4: SETTING GOALS

"Setting goals is the first step in turning
the invisible into the visible."
~*Tony Robbins*

If you have already signed up to take an online class...congratulations! That means you have already set a goal for yourself. It may be as simple as passing one course. That's fine. It's a step in the right direction. It is very important to have not only educational goals but also personal goals. The mistake that many people make when setting goals is that they usually do not make them sufficiently measurable so they can hold themselves accountable.

Making Goals Measurable

Think about the typical goals that people have. Let's say you want to lose weight. That's a goal many people share. Just saying you want to lose weight is not going to make it happen, though. You have to cut back on your calories, maybe exercise more, etc. Even then, just saying you will eat less and exercise more is not a very specific or measurable way to set a goal. The goal will be much easier to attain if you specify the amount of calories you will intake. You will need to identify healthy foods you will be eating, rather than saying something vague like I'm going to eat less. To stay within those limits you may state you will eat a specific amount of oatmeal and bananas for breakfast, tuna and brown rice for lunch, chicken and steamed vegetables for dinner on Mondays, something similarly healthy on Tuesdays, etc. You might also mention what exercise you will do to achieve those goals. Perhaps you will exercise by including 30 minutes of walking on Mondays, swimming on Wednesdays and cycling on Fridays. By getting specific, you have set the calorie intake and output you are aiming for in order to lose weight.

Being specific is just as important when setting educational goals. Let's say I want to graduate with a Bachelor of Science degree in four years. Just saying that alone is not specific enough to really ensure that it happens. I need to create shorter, more measurable steps along the way. I might decide that I need to sign up for 15 credits a semester, choosing from those that are listed on the packet of required courses that my counselor gave me. I might also decide that I will study on Monday, Wednesday and Friday nights from 6 pm to 8 pm, and mark those times off in my calendar. I could also decide that I will use from 5 pm to 7 pm on Sunday nights to plan what needs to be done for the coming week's assignments. By getting very specific with the tasks that are required in order to meet my goals, I am far more likely to reach those goals.

Goals are an important thing to have in your life. Think about it...you can just exist, and go on doing the same old thing day after day, or you can have a purpose... some particular thing or things you want to reach for or attain in your life. Creating both short-term and long-term goals or things you want to achieve in life gives you something to look forward to, and something to celebrate when they occur. Too often, I hear older students tell me they wish they had gone to school a long time ago. Many times, they just never had anyone push them, or they simply never realized the importance of it.

Having Foresight

Part of being a successful person or running a successful business is having foresight. Having long-term goals means you've thought about your future, and are working to attain a better life. I teach many different levels of business-related courses, and in those courses, we invariably discuss the importance of proactive change. Think about it. What stresses people out? Unanticipated change is a biggy! But if you are thinking with foresight, and considering all the possible things that could happen, you are being proactive, and not just reacting to change. That puts you in the driver's seat.

Many people may ask themselves, "How high should I aim"? The answer to that will vary for each individual, and there's no point in comparing yourself with anyone else. You need to aim for *your* best, not someone else's best. If the best you have ever done in school was a C, it may not be reasonable to expect to get straight A's in your first semester. That doesn't mean that you won't eventually reach that point, but perhaps it is more reasonable to try for a B first. Sometimes, it takes time to be our best that we can be. The most important thing is that we are continually working on being better. So, if you get into an online class and see that there are other students in there who seem to know it all and have a handle on things, that doesn't mean you should know it as well as they do. You don't know what experiences they may or may not have had. You just need to do the best you can do.

Self-Analysis

Something that can be very helpful in setting your goals and understanding your abilities is what the business world calls a SWOT analysis. SWOT stands for Strengths, Weaknesses, Opportunities and Threats. In the corporate setting, leaders analyze their organizations in terms of these areas, but it is a good exercise for individuals to do as well. Think about those areas where you have strengths. Write them down. Perhaps you have great writing skills. Perhaps you are tenacious. Now think about your weaknesses. Write them down. Perhaps you don't have strong technology skills. Perhaps you lack motivation. Now write down your opportunities. Perhaps this degree will lead to a promotion. Perhaps you will now learn computer skills that you never had before. Lastly, write down your threats. Perhaps you have limited funds to pay for your classes. Perhaps you do not have your family's support in going back to school.

Now that you have written all of this down, write down the solutions to your weaknesses and threats. Using the previous examples, how can you improve your technological skills? Maybe you can watch a tutorial or buy a book. How can you get more funds to pay for college? Maybe you could check for scholarships or employer funding. When setting your goals, pay special attention to your positives, i.e. your strengths and opportunities, and work on your weaknesses and threats. See the appendix at the back of the book for a sample SWOT analysis form.

The key to going to school and finishing that degree is being tenacious and not giving up. Think about people you know who have made it through college. A lot of what got them through was that they were able to develop endurance, and didn't give up. You'd be surprised just how quickly four years goes by. The sooner you begin your education, the sooner you will have your diploma.

CHAPTER 5: TIME MANAGEMENT

"Efficiency is doing things right.
Effectiveness is doing the right things."
~Peter Drucker

When we think about time management, one of the first things we need to decide is how much time we have to do the things we want to do. The answer is that we have the same amount of time as everyone else. Webster has many definitions for time, such as, "The hours or days required to be occupied by one's work" or "a period during which something is used or available for use." What we accomplish in life, all depends on how we choose to use our time.

Making Time Tangible

I would like to challenge your view of time, and encourage you to make it more tangible, more visual and measurable. Organize time like you would space.

Think of tasks in terms of how they would fit into the given space. When you are organizing your closet, you make room for your shoes, right? If you rearrange your closet, you can find room for more shoes. Believe me, there is always room for more shoes! We need to think of time in a similar way to how we think about space.

Time is our most critical resource, and for most of us, it's scarce. No one seems to have enough, yet everyone has all there is! According to time management expert Alan Lakein, "To waste your time is to waste your life, but to master your time is to master your life and make the most of it" (Lakein, 1974). You get 86,400 seconds each day, and you cannot save any of them. When you say you do not have time to do something, you are really saying that you value some other event or activity more. How often do we convince ourselves we don't have time? What we really mean is that we have allowed insignificant events like watching TV to become more important than writing that book we've always wanted to write. Want to know what Jack Bauer is going to do tonight? Record it and watch it later, maybe as a reward for completing your assignment. No one is saying you can't watch TV once in a while, but if you watch your TV shows while you exercise, then you are saving time by multi-tasking. That gives you more time to do other things, like study for school.

What are You Trying to Achieve?

It is interesting that in many time-management classes they jump right in and talk about how to manage your day-to-day activities. Managing your time on a daily basis is important, but there is another important piece to the puzzle. What are you using your time to achieve?

Yogi Bera is often quoted as saying, "If you don't know where you are going, you'll end up someplace else." You may have an idea of some things you would like to accomplish, in fact you may have even written some of them down. Make sure that everything you do is in some way related to achieving your goals. If you are planning to take on online course, think about where you want that course to lead. Do you want to graduate? What degree do you want to obtain? What will you do with that degree?

Roadblocks

What is holding you back from achieving your goals? Do you need a skill or technique that you currently do not have? Are you miscalculating how long things take? Through practice, you can become a better time esti-mator. Do you need special training in some subject that you haven't had in order to be more efficient? Perhaps you don't feel sufficiently skilled with computer software or in utilizing Word programs. What can you do to improve that? Do you have other issues such as a medical problem that results in you being tired all the time? Adjust your expectations and give yourself a break.

There can be all sorts of psychological roadblocks. Some people have difficulty with time management because they feel a need for perfection. Nothing ever seems to get finished, because it is never good enough for them. Step back and look at your situation. Do you have a fear of failure, or maybe even a fear of success? Perhaps you just thrive on chaos. I see a lot of people who aren't happy unless they have major dramas going on in their life. Maybe it spices things up for them. They could even be self-sabotaging for the drama it brings. Which one is more helpful for your future? Having drama in your life, or having a college degree?

Everyone has a different way of managing their time. We all have preferences about when or how we do certain tasks or activities. If you like a fast pace, you'll fill your day with numerous activities. If you like a slower pace, limit your to-do list to just a few items. If you schedule too much, it will work against you.

Many factors can affect your ability to accomplish tasks. Think about your energy levels at different times of the day. If you are a morning person, for example, allocate your time to do important things early in the day. Save the less important things for when your energy level is lower. Ups and downs in your energy levels can have a profound effect on your ability to finish the things on your to-do list. Eating on the run, heat, monotony, medications, etc. can all affect your performance. Give your brain a break from time to time by doing a task that requires you to move around, and then give your body a break by being still and using your brain.

What are You Avoiding?

What things fail to motivate you? Sometimes, we avoid doing certain things. We think we might fail, or someone might get mad at us, or maybe we have had a bad experience with this activity in the past. I used to have a sales job where I was required to cold-call all day long. No one wants to be told "no", or to be hung up on…it can be demotivating, if not downright terrifying, so using positive self-talk is critical to getting yourself past this obstacle. If I told myself that the guy was going to hang up on me, which would upset me, that wasn't going to motivate me to call him. If, on the other hand, I told myself, "I will learn something from the next call, even if he hangs up on me. I can do it. I can do it now!" I would be motivated to continue.

It's the same with going to school. You might fail a class, which is always possible. Does that mean you should just give up and tell yourself you were not meant for class? No. It just means you need to plan better for when you take the course again. You will have learned a lot from taking the course the first time, and hopefully that will be the last time it happens.

Staying Motivated

How do you stay motivated to succeed? Always try to find someone who does things better than you, and watch them. What do they do differently? Multi-tasking might be the thing that makes it possible for them to accomplish all the things they do. Notice what tricks other people use to get things done, and try to incorporate some of them into your daily routine. At first, this might not be easy, but once you get used to it, you'll find you've got more time for activities like studying.

Prioritizing

Many students have a busy work schedule, and there are many thoughts on how best to deal with all the stuff people have to look at on a daily basis at work. One of the best things I have run across is a plan by David Allen, the author of Getting Things Done (2002). In his plan, the first thing that needs to be done is to decide what to do with stuff you need to deal with. Once something is put into your in-box, what do you do with it? It has been said that you should never touch a piece of paper twice. In other words, if it needs to be filed, do it. Do not wait and put it in a pending file to be looked at later. Look at what it is, and see if it needs action. If no action is needed, throw it away, file it, or keep it for later reference. If action is needed, then you need to decide if it will take more than two minutes. If not, then just do it. If so, then it needs to be either delegated or deferred to another time. If deferred, then it must be scheduled.

One you learn how to be organized, it is easy to attain your goals. Remember, you must write your goals down, and then break them down into more specific interim targets. If your goal is to graduate, make a list of the steps needed to get there. What activities will be required to reach that goal? Set realistic timelines. For example, you cannot expect to graduate in one year, but you can in four. Have checkpoints set up along the way. Perhaps after six months you might reevaluate your goal. Maybe initially you thought you wanted to get a communications degree, but after taking a business course, you might decide to change your major. Now you will need to change the steps required to get to your new goal. You will need to take different classes, etc. If you have to adjust your timeline, do it...make the necessary adjustments before it is too late.

Every day, we prioritize (consciously or unconsciously). How we prioritize tasks is important. Look what you have written down, and think about the order in which these steps must be taken to accomplish your goal. By writing things down, it makes it easier to see how to get to your goal, but always keep in mind that things do come up unexpectedly, so don't beat yourself up if you cannot meet your forecasted deadlines.

Plan for the Unplanned

It is important to plan for the unplanned. Allow some time each day for unplanned or urgent activities. Also be realistic in the amount of time you allocate for your planned activities. At first, it may be hard to judge how much time you require, but the amount should decrease over time as you learn to multi-task and become more productive. Many people underestimate how much time it actually takes to do certain planned activities. Your goal may be to do something in three hours, but after spending two hours on the task, you find that it is going to take you longer than you thought. Perhaps you forgot to include an hour of preparation time. Always factor in more than the minimum estimated amount of time. Figure out the time you think it will take to do something, and then add an extra 20% into your schedule.

The Pareto Principle

Many of you probably have heard of the Pareto Principle, whereby 80% of your actions or efforts contribute to only 20% of your actual results, while 20% of your actions or efforts yield 80% of your results. The message is, 80% of what you are working on may not be very productive. There are a lot of things we do that simply steal our time and rob us of our success. Look at something as simple as managing email. We could spend all day just going through all the stuff we get at home or at work. Remember to look at everything just once, make a brief response if possible, flag it if it is important, and then move on. Too many people waste time sitting and thinking about each email. It is important to be able to bring the same efficient approach to other areas of your life in order to free up time for your school work.

Setting a Schedule

I always recommend that students set up schedules to follow. Get a day timer or a calendar of some sort and enter all your scheduled activities. If your plan is to study from 6 to 8 pm on Mondays, Wednesdays, and Fridays, be sure to write that down in your planner. One way to know what will be required of you is to print out the syllabus from the courses you are taking. The syllabus should show the due dates for every activity. As soon as you become aware of when items are due, write down not only the due date, but also the dates on which you will be working to complete that assignment. Try not to leave it until the night before they are due to tackle assignments. You need to be thinking with foresight. There may be issues with the Internet or the Web site. What happens if you wait until the last minute to submit your assignment and your computer crashes? As far as the school and the professor are concerned, you're out of luck. It's not their problem that you didn't plan ahead to allow for the unexpected. Many professors allow you to submit assignments early. Whenever this is permitted, I would recommend doing so. Always try to keep one step ahead.

Remember to also include some downtime into your schedule. If you plan too many activities, you will burn out, so schedule a little downtime. Remember, there should be a work–life balance. If you have children, it is not realistic to schedule your study time right when they are going to be at their most alert, and wanting your attention. The key to having a successful time management plan is to make it reasonable. If you make it too difficult to stick to, you won't follow through.

Track Your Day

I suggest that you track what you do during a typical 24-hour day, in fact I would suggest doing this for several days to see how you are spending most of your time. Sometimes, by writing down our daily activities, we are better able to focus on those things that we are doing that are actually wasting our time. Create a chart like the one listed in the Appendix at the back of the book and spend a day or two writing down what you do during the day. Be specific. Don't simply write "working" or "household activities". The more specific you are, the more you can see precisely where you are spending your time. When you are finished with this activity, think about where you are wasting time. What can you change in your day? Are your goals being met by your activities? How can you incorporate your goals into your day? See an example of a time management sheet in the Appendix at the back of the book.

I have had students do this exercise in many of the courses I have taught, and I always find it interesting that the ones who have the most excuses for why they are late with assignments turn in a sample day of activities showing quite a bit of television watching or telephone chatting. These are the ones who seem to have the best excuses for being late. Some students are used to people not really holding them accountable for their actions, and they get very upset when a professor doesn't allow them to turn in their assignments late.

Reasonable Excuses

Remember, professors usually list their late policy on the first day of class. It is very important to read this so you're familiar with their rules. Emergencies sometimes arise; indeed I have had emergencies come up both while being a student and a professor. I am fortunate in the fact that I have a laptop computer that I can take anywhere with me should the need arise, however many students don't have this luxury.

If you are sick, or have family issues, it is very important that you make the professor aware of this as soon as the situation arises. I have worked with plenty of students who have had some serious issues come up in their lives, and I'm very sympathetic to that, as I have had some of my own issues and can relate to the difficulties that they bring.

However, keep in mind that what you may see as a reasonable excuse may not really qualify as an emergency, or as an acceptable reason for late submission of work. I remember having one student in the not-too-distant past who was not the most tactful student in class. She had a lot of excuses for being late, and would get very angry if she lost any points for her tardiness. I remember one time she was quite upset that her air conditioning had gone out, and said that she was unable to post her assignment because of it. Now, I live in Arizona, so I have great sympathy for anyone dealing with air-conditioning issues, however that is not an acceptable excuse for being late. Interestingly, when I asked her where she was from, it was a state not known for its heat.

I have had my own health issues during times when I have been teaching, in fact during one semester, I had two stays in hospital and some pretty major complications. I never missed any days of work though, because I worked from my hospital bed. Okay, so I'm a bit over the top...however, during this time, I received notes from students, often many days after a paper was due, saying they could not turn in their assignment due to having a sore throat, or some other minor ailment. I would type my response from my hospital bed, trying to be sympathetic, and yet firmly explaining that we all have life's issues come up, and we need to learn to deal with them. My point is, be reasonable with your expectations and excuses. If you really do have an emergency, or have someone in your family who is very ill, that is a good reason to be late. If you have a cold, or have had a hard week at work, that's just part of life. My best advice would be to do your work as soon as you know what is assigned. It is better to have your homework finished early and be ready to post it than to wait until the last minute and have life's issues get in the way.

Staying Organized

If you complete your assignments early, it shows that you're probably an organized person. It's just that some people are more organized than others. It is claimed that we get our abilities through both nature and nurture, so if you feel that you haven't been born with organizational skills, it is never too late to work on it. Just be careful not to make the mistake of planning too much. I have seen the guy who plans the plan to plan the plan and never actually gets anything done except for a lot of planning!

There are several things you can do to become more organized prior to attending your first online class. You have already taken a big step by choosing to read this book. By doing so, you already have a good idea of how to get around online and a better understanding of the terminology you will confront before you've even attended a class.

As I have noted previously, the first thing you need to do is to print out your class syllabus. This is tells you what the teacher expects, grade scales, objectives, and sometimes includes the homework assignments. I would recommend posting the syllabus somewhere near your computer. I would also take any dates that are listed on it and enter those into your planner or day timer. Remember, you should not only include the date that the assignment is due, but also block out time for when you will work on that assignment.

If you are taking multiple classes online, I would recommend keeping notebooks for each class. I currently teach for six different online universities. To keep their rules and requirements straight in my mind, I have a different notebook for each of those universities. I would recommend you do the same thing for each of your courses. You may find that you spend more time getting organized for your first class, since it is a new experience, but as you take more online classes, this will take up less of your time.

One of the nice things about an online class is that all of the information about that class is portable. In other words, you can access it from work or you can access it from home. This is extremely helpful in the event of a computer crashing. You can always get online at the library or using a friend's computer should this happen. Even if you've left your syllabus at home, you'll be able to access it online.

One trick I have learned in relation to doing homework is to do the things that I hate first. If I have to do two things that are both due on the same day, I will always do the one I hate first. That leaves me with the good feeling of knowing that the bad thing is now out of the way, and the only thing left to do is the easier or more pleasant thing.

There may be times when you only have time to do one of two things. In such cases, be sure that the one you choose is worth the most points. Many students make the mistake of doing the easier thing, which is worth fewer points, and then run out of time to do something that is worth a lot more. That is not to say you cannot turn in things late. Most professors have a policy of accepting late papers with a penalty. Do not make the mistake of thinking that because you missed the due date, there's no point in turning anything in. It is better to lose 10% for being one day late than to get a zero for not turning in any work at all.

When you do begin to study, it is important that you read the following chapter on increasing retention. Many students know how to highlight texts or to use flashcards to some extent, however there are many more techniques available out there to help you to increase your retention of the material you are studying.

CHAPTER 6: MOTIVATION

"Success is not final, failure is not fatal: it is
the courage to continue that counts."
~*Winston Churchill*

What is motivation? There are many ways to define this. It can be an internal excitement about doing something. Many refer to it as having drive or desire. It can be thought of as a force directing behavior. Some of it is intrinsic, or contained within you, while some of it is extrinsic, based upon external forces. However you define motivation, it is something that many students need to work on developing.

Although you might be fortunate enough to find teachers who have read all of the books about motivating their students and are willing to set a fire under you to help you succeed, chances are you will need to develop some internal motivation. You might think that just because you have found the motivation to sign up for your first online course this will be all that is necessary.

However, it is important for online students understand that there will be good days and bad days, just like with any other school, job, relationship, etc. Therefore, it is important to have realistic expectations and goals.

Incentives

Sometimes, you will have built-in incentives for you in terms of grades, achievement, and so on. However, I also recommend that you provide some external incentives to motivate you. Perhaps you will promise yourself a night out, or a nice dinner, if you pass the course. Or you may decide that if you study a certain number of hours a week, you deserve that new pair of shoes. Sometimes, external incentives can motivate people as much as the grades or other incentives that are intrinsic to the course itself.

Your home environment can often be either a source of motivation or contribute to a lack of motivation. I have had students who haven't really had the support of their families, but I've also had students whose families are cheering them on. If your family is happy and positive about your decision to go back to school, this can be a strong motivation. If your family is not as supportive, it may help with your motivation to avoid them during your study time. Perhaps you can go to a library to study, or go outside to read.

Realistic Expectations

What is important is that students have realistic expectations. If you believe that you will only be successful if you get a 4.0, then you are setting yourself up to fail. If you have never had any experience with computers and you expect to learn it all the first day, again, you are setting yourself up to fail. You must be realistic, and understand that no one is perfect. There will be a variety of students in the course, some who are smarter than you and others who aren't, some who are more technologically savvy than you others who aren't. Try not to compare yourself to anyone else. If you are being the best that you can be, that is what is important.

Part of becoming demotivated stems from frustration due to lack of knowledge, and many students find themselves in this position because they do not ask questions. One of the nicest things about online learning is that you can ask questions privately in your individual area of the class, where no one can see it but the professor. Don't hesitate to ask about anything you think you need help with. Many students are afraid of looking stupid, but you will not look stupid. Professors are there to answer your questions – that's their job. That's not to say you won't get the occasional professor who answers in a snippy tone, but don't let that get you down. Sometimes, people just are having a bad day. You might get a professor who isn't blessed with the best personality, but that's their problem, not yours. Even if they give you a snippy answer, it's still an answer. Don't let their negativity get to you. Sometimes, people are just cranky. It has nothing to do with you. And remember, as was discussed earlier, sometimes the way we type our messages, including answers to questions, doesn't show the inflection of meaning as well as it might. What is important is that you get your answer. If the professor is grumpy, you'll probably only have them for one course, anyway. Just as with any other schools, there will be the nice teachers and the cranky ones. It's up to you to realize that, to accept it, and not be afraid to ask questions as necessary.

Prioritize

Set your priorities early. Remember to read the section on goal setting. It's important that you place your education as a priority, but you also have to be realistic regarding your job and/or your other responsibilities. Don't beat yourself up if you have to submit an assignment late because of work or family obligations. The important thing to remember is that you have learned the material. The fact that you were one day late, which maybe cost you a few points, depending on the system being used, is relatively unimportant.

Stay Connected

One good way to stay motivated is to feel a sense of belonging to the group, in this case your fellow students. The chat rooms are there for a reason. You can post anything (clean) that you want in there that is respectful of others. If you want to talk about the game that was on TV last night, you can do it there. Extend the friendship branch. You will be surprised at how many others want to talk as well.

Some Anxiety is Normal

Always remember that a certain amount of anxiety is not necessarily a bad thing, and can serve to drive us at times. That little anxious feeling in our stomach telling us that we need to get our paper in on time motivates us to not procrastinate. Don't worry if you feel a little bit of apprehension – that is normal for any student. Many students who haven't been online in a long time have even greater anxiety about technology and things they feel they are not as familiar with as others. Instead of telling yourself that you are behind the curve and can't learn new things, tell yourself that this is your opportunity to become tech savvy!

Remember, motivation is largely about our attitudes. Do you look at the cup as half empty or half full? If you have traditionally been a half-empty kind of person, think about where that has gotten you in this world. It is never too late to change how we perceive things. If we have reasonable expectations, we are more likely to succeed.

Maintaining Enthusiasm

It is very important to work on keeping up your level of enthusiasm. It would be nice to have Tony Robbins in your home every day cheering you on, however this is not realistic. Therefore, you need to work on your enthusiasm. If it doesn't come naturally to you, perhaps you can set it as one of your goals. Write in your calendar each day that you will make one enthusiastic comment to someone that day. Developing enthusiasm is just like any other habit. The more you do it, the more it becomes ingrained.

Learning is More Important than the Grade

I also cannot stress enough how important it is for you to master the subject rather than obtaining the perfect grade. I would rather get a C and learn something than get an A and learn nothing. You are going back to school for a reason. If you want to better yourself, part of that is mastering new knowledge. I have met plenty of A students who are not necessarily the brightest people. They may be more tenacious, and have the drive to get good grades, but that doesn't mean they have learned the material as well as the student in their class who got a B–.

Ask for Help!

If you need individualized attention, don't be afraid to ask for extra help. Your professor might be able to answer all of your questions, or they might also be able to recommend some additional reading. I mentor or teach a lot of doctoral students, and I see a wide variety in terms of need for help and attention even with students at this high level. It is never a sign of weakness to ask for help. In fact, I see it as the student having a strong desire to succeed. Just as with a regular face-to-face classroom, teachers cannot be expected to be available 24/7, however most professors list certain hours when they can be contacted, and many universities have a policy that questions should be answered within 24 hours.

Look for Challenges

Sometimes, a good way to stay motivated is to look for challenges. Perhaps you will find that the first few classes are mostly a review of things you already know. That's okay. Utilize this time to get back into the school routine. Perhaps you can take more than a course or two at a time. Each school has different rules. I always liked to go along at a very fast pace. I would look at the syllabus as soon as I could get my hands on it, establish when all the assignments were due and then do all of the work at the beginning. If you adopt this approach, you may have to wait to actually submit your assignments, but when the submission date comes around, they will already be done, and you will have challenged yourself in the process.

Others may find that they are not so much looking for more challenges as relief from the stress they are experiencing. There will be stressful times, undoubtedly. Sometimes, visualizing the thing that is stressing you out, as well as the solution, can be helpful. Always focus on the positive, and evaluate the situation to see which things you could have done better. Seek out other on-line learners with whom you can share your experiences. If you are an older student, and don't see yourself as technology-oriented, you might find it helpful to take some online tutorials to learn some of the software programs out there.

Studying at home does not necessarily mean studying in isolation. There are a lot of people out there who you can go to for help. Keep in mind there are counselors, professors, fellow students, online tutorials, friends, co-workers and family who can provide support. If you are the type who enjoys working or being alone, you'll probably enjoy studying online. If you like to have a lot of interaction, you can create that for yourself as well.

The most motivating aspect of online learning may simply be to have fun. Enjoy what you are learning. Listen to your fellow students' experiences, and share yours with them. The great diversity of students undertaking online learning will make this sharing experience much more interesting than you might have expected. And remember to enjoy your successes. When things are going well, give yourself a pat on the back for a job well done.

CHAPTER 7:
INCREASING RETENTION

"I admit that Post-it note sheets that adhere to virtually any surface are now my substitute choice for retention."
~Candice Bergen

What is reading retention? Basically, it is the ability to remember or recall the things that you have read. When you read, your mind has to understand the words that you read. It sounds easy, doesn't it? Unfortunately, many of us were not really taught the correct way to maximize our reading retention. There is a common quote, the original author of which is unknown, that says, "We retain 10 percent of what we read, 20 percent of what we hear, 30 percent of what we see, 70 percent of what we say, and 90 percent of what we say and do." Whether it is true or not, one thing is certain – people often have to read something several times to get a good grasp of the concepts contained therein.

Many students get frustrated right off the bat when they are studying because they make one or more of the following mistakes. They may assume they can learn the material by reading an article or book chapter just once. They may not know what certain words mean, and may not bother to look them up. They may also neglect to try to see connections or patterns in the information that they are reading.

Proper Reading Speed

It's important to keep in mind that reading a text is not like reading a novel, but it can be just as interesting. If you assume something is going to be boring before you read it, you have closed your mind to the possibilities of learning. Reading for study purposes requires more concentration, so it is important to find a quiet location where there are minimal distractions. It's also important not to rush through the material too quickly. You should always base your reading speed on the type of material you are reading:

Texts and Technical Journals – slow
Manuals and Nonfiction – slow to medium
Magazines – medium to fast
Fiction – faster

Reading something quickly just so you can say you got through it is not the same as reading to gain a real understanding of the material. Having said that, you can increase your reading speed through practice. First, time yourself to see how fast you currently read. To figure out your speed, read a page of average text and write down the time it took you to read it. Let's say it took you 3 minutes and 15 seconds, which can be expressed as 3.25 minutes in decimals. Now count the number of words on the page you just read. Let's say there were 325 words on the page. If you divide that by the 3.25 minutes it took you to read the page, it will give you your reading speed, which in this case is 100 words per minute. Make a note of your speed, and check it every six months to see if you are improving.

Now, think about what you just read. Can you remember the details? If someone was to quiz you about what was on that page, how would you do? If you retained the information, you are reading at a good speed, and should feel confident trying to improve upon it, while still retaining the meaning. If, however, you can't remember what you just read, you may be rushing you reading. Try reading it again, more slowly this time, paying closer attention to what you are reading. Take note of whether you find yourself speaking the words you are reading out loud, or if you can hear them in your head. Vocalizing what you are reading actually slows you down. If your goal is to increase your speed, try to avoid speaking the words.

Vocabulary

Perhaps you are being slowed down by some of the vocabulary in the text you are reading. It is very important to build your vocabulary. Buy a couple of cheap dictionaries and keep them handy. Every time you read a word you don't understand, look it up. You might also purchase one of those word-a-day calendars to help you learn new words, although sometimes these can be unusual, rarely used words. The best way to build your vocabulary is to write down any words you don't know whenever you encounter them and look them up as you go.

Spelling and Grammar

In my online courses, I see a lot of students who have poor spelling and grammar. Many of them rely on spell-check to solve their spelling problems. Unfortunately, spell-check does not catch every error, and sometimes it even suggests a word that may be completely wrong. Although it is a good idea to use spell-check, do not automatically assume that it is giving you the right answer in the case of words you do not use a lot. If you're not familiar with the word spell-check has suggested, look it up in a dictionary. Many people misspell the following words: calendar, embarrass, questionnaire, accommodate and definitely. For a list of some of the other most commonly misspelled words, check out the following: http://www.yourdictionary.com/library/misspelled.html.

Many students also struggle with basic grammar issues. Some of the biggest mistakes I see include starting sentences with the word "Me", or using the words "Me" and "I" incorrectly. For example, you should never say something like, "Me and Bob went to the movies." It should be, "Bob and I went to the movies." What happens then, though, is students hear that and think they should use "I" instead of "Me" for everything, but that is not correct. For example, you should never say, "It was a good year for Bob and I." It should be, "It was a good year for Bob and me." An easy way to check if you are writing it correctly is to remove the words "Bob and" from the sentence. Now it says, "It was a good year for me." That is correct. You would not say, "It was a good year for I."

Because online students have Internet access, I highly recommend checking out the following link: http://grammar.quickanddirtytips.com/. On this site, "Grammar Girl" gives lots of tips about how to speak and write correctly. There are Grammar Girl podcasts that are available on Itunes as well. The author does a nice job of educating people about grammar in a fun and entertaining way!

Study Techniques to Improve Retention

Now that you have worked on your spelling and grammar, there are some other ways to help you with your reading retention. Many schools have students study something called SQ3R. That stands for Survey, Question, Read, Recite and Review. For more information about SQ3R, check out http://www.studytechniques.org/reading-styles-strategies.html. The process includes going over what you will be reading, or previewing it, so that you know what to expect when you actually start to read it. Think of it as setting the stage so that there won't be any surprises. You should look at the table of contents, all of the chapter headings, and the indexes, and then check to see if there are any other sections of the book that might require your attention.

Once you have surveyed what you will be reading, it is time to question it. Think about what the assignment you will be submitting actually requires. Formulate questions in your head about what types of things you should be looking for in your reading. Sometimes you can think up questions based on looking at headings or subheadings in chapters. Have questions in mind that you want to have answered as you are reading the text.

As you begin the first part of the 3Rs, reading, think about those questions. Take notes and highlight your text as you go along. Don't highlight just for the sake of it, and don't highlight everything, just the important points that you may want to go back to later. If you need to fold down corners on the text, I recommend doing that. My husband hates it when I do that, and says I am destroying the book. However, I find it very helpful to be able to quickly tab back to areas of importance later. If you're reluctant to fold corners, perhaps you could insert page markers, preferably sticky ones, like Post-it flags, so they don't fall out. It is your book, so make the best use of it!

The second R is recite. Think about the answers you were looking for in the assignment, and say those answers out loud. Think about how it sounds. Does what you are saying make sense? You may find that you want to stop after just a few paragraphs and recite your answer based on what you have read so far, or you may feel you can wait until the end of a section. Practice with this to see how much you can retain. You may find that you have to reread the material to be able to truly digest it sufficiently to be able to recite what you have learned.

The last R is review. I suggest that you do this right away, and several more times as well if you are going to be tested on the material. Reviewing may take the form of looking at your notes, seeing if you can answer the questions that have been posed, self-quizzing, or just discussing what you have read with someone else.

Now that you have learned some important techniques for retention, it is important to understand that we all have different personalities, and may require different strategies for learning based upon these personality styles.

CHAPTER 8: PERSONALITIES

"Always be yourself, express yourself, have faith
in yourself...do not go out and look for a
successful personality and duplicate it."
~Bruce Lee

In the book *The Young Adult's Guide to Understanding Personalities* that I wrote with my daughter Toni, we discuss the importance of understanding personalities. Your personality may be seen as your social reputation, or the way in which others perceive you. However, there is also the unseen part of what makes you distinctly different in terms of your behavior and how you react to things. Understanding your personality can be important for the online student. Based upon our personality, we tend to have different strengths when it comes to our types of intelligence.

Types of Intelligence

You're probably very familiar with the term IQ, which stands for intelligence quotient, but there are many other types of intelligence. In fact, I wrote my doctoral dissertation about something called Emotional Intelligence. Emotional intelligence, simply defined, is having an understanding of your own emotions as well as those of others. When considering our types of intelligence when it comes to learning, there are several areas where we may or may not excel. These include:

"Verbal-Linguistic – The verbal style involves both the written and spoken word. If you use this style, you find it easy to express yourself, both in writing and verbally. You love reading and writing. You like playing on the meaning or sound of words, such as in tongue twisters, rhymes, limericks and the like. You know the meaning of many words, and regularly make an effort to find the meaning of new words. You use these words, as well as phrases you have picked up recently, when talking to others." (learning-styles-online.com, 2010)

"Logical-Mathematical – If you use the logical style, you like using your brain for logical and mathematical reasoning. You can recognize patterns easily, as well as connections between seemingly meaningless content. This also leads you to classify and group information to help you learn or understand it. You typically work through problems and issues in a systematic way, and you like to create procedures for future use. You are happy setting numerical targets and budgets, and you track your progress towards these. You like creating agendas, itineraries, and to-do lists, and you typically number and rank them before putting them into action." (learning-styles-online.com, 2010)

"Bodily-Kinesthetic – ability to control body move-ments and handle objects skillfully. These learners ex-press themselves through movement. They have a good sense of balance and eye–hand co-ordination. (e.g., ball play, balancing beams). Through interacting with the space around them, they are able to remember and process information." (IDpride.net, 2010)

"Visual-Spatial – ability to perceive the visual. These learners tend to think in pictures and need to create vivid mental images to retain information. They enjoy looking at maps, charts, pictures, videos, and movies. Their skills include: puzzle building, reading, writing, understanding charts and graphs, a good sense of direction, sketching, painting, creating visual metaphors and analogies (per-haps through the visual arts), manipulating images, con-structing, fixing, designing practical objects, interpreting visual images." (IDpride.net, 2010)

"Interpersonal (also called social) – If you have a strong social style, you communicate well with people, both verbally and non-verbally. People listen to you or come to you for advice, and you are sensitive to their motivations, feelings or moods. You listen well and un-derstand other's views. You may enjoy mentoring or counseling others. You typically prefer learning in groups or classes, or you like to spend much one-on-one time with a teacher or an instructor. You heighten your learning by bouncing your thoughts off other people and listening to how they respond. You prefer to work through issues, ideas and problems with a group. You thoroughly enjoy working with a "clicking" or synergistic group of people." (learning-styles-online.com, 2010)

"Intrapersonal (also called solitary) – If you have a solitary style, you are more private, introspective and independent. You can concentrate well, focusing your thoughts and feelings on your current topic. You are aware of your own thinking, and you may analyze the different ways you think and feel. You spend time on self-analysis, and often reflect on past events and the way you approached them. You take time to ponder and assess your own accomplishments or challenges. You may keep a journal, diary or personal log to record your personal thoughts and events." (learning-styles-online.com, 2010)

"Musical-rhythmic (also called Aural) – If you use the aural style, you like to work with sound and music. You have a good sense of pitch and rhythm. You typically can sing, play a musical instrument, or identify the sounds of different instruments. Certain music invokes strong emotions. You notice the music playing in the background of movies, TV shows and other media. You often find yourself humming or tapping a song or jingle, or a theme or jingle pops into your head without prompting." (learning-styles-online.com, 2010)

"Naturalistic – Naturalist intelligence designates the human ability to discriminate among living things (plants, animals) as well as sensitivity to other features of the natural world (clouds, rock configurations). This ability was clearly of value in our evolutionary past as hunters, gatherers, and farmers; it continues to be central in such roles as botanist or chef. The kind of pattern recognition valued in certain sciences may also draw upon the naturalist intelligence." (chariho.k12.ri.us, 2010)

Think about the definitions of these different intelligence types. Do you see yourself within one of these areas? Sometimes we are strong in several areas. What is important to understand is how certain strategies work best for certain types of learning abilities or intelligences. For example, you might find that the following strategies are helpful for various types of intelligence:

> Verbal-Linguistic – Does well with the SQ3R. They should take a lot of notes.
> Logical-Mathematical – Think about how things relate while you are reading. You probably prefer to start at chapter one and proceed in order, rather than jump around.

Bodily-Kinesthetic – Pace yourself, and take breaks to do something active to break things up.

Visual-Spatial – Look at tables, pictures and other visual items on the page. Sometimes creating charts for yourself can be helpful.

Interpersonal – Study with a friend. Talk to others about what you have learned.

Intrapersonal – You probably do your best studying in solitude. Think about how what you just read impacts you.

Musical-rhythmic – Perhaps you study better with music playing. Create musical rhythms or songs to help you remember key concepts.

Naturalistic – Maybe you would prefer to study outdoors. If you cannot do that, picture yourself in an outdoor setting to relax yourself.

Introvert vs. Extrovert

By understanding our own personality characteristics, we can better relate to our fellow classmates as well. There is a very popular personality test out there called the Myers–Briggs assessment. This test can tell you what your basic preferences are when it comes to how you take in information. I used to teach organizations to utilize this information to help their corporate teams work well together. By understanding why people act the way they do, it is easier for them to get along together better. This is not only helpful for organizations, but has uses within the classroom setting as well.

One of the main parts of our personality as defined by the Myers–Briggs indicator is whether we are introverts or extroverts. You may have heard these terms before. Many think of extroverts as talkative and introverts as quiet people, but that is not necessarily true. Being an introvert or an extrovert is more about how you process information. If you are an introvert, you tend to take in information and think internally before you speak. If you are an extrovert, you tend to take in information and process it externally, meaning you say what you are thinking. Therefore, it may appear that an extrovert talks a lot, but they are actually just thinking out loud. It may appear that an introvert is quiet, but they are probably simply processing what you just said to them.

I have found that certain schools where I work have a lot of introverts in the classroom. I have never seen an actual study on the percentages of online students that are introverts vs. extroverts, but it would be an interesting study. For those of you who are introverted and like to take your time to formulate answers, online is a wonderful place to do that. Think about the pressure that is removed for the introvert in online learning. In a face-to-face setting, the instructor may come up to the introvert and ask them a question. Because they feel pressure to answer, this can be very uncomfortable. Online learn-ing gives the introvert more time to gather their thoughts and provide a suitable response.

What is nice for the extrovert in the online environ-ment is that they may avoid blurting out something they later wish they hadn't. By typing out their responses and having time to edit them, they can avoid saying too much or saying something they haven't had time to fully develop. I am an extrovert, and find the online atmosphere helpful in another regard. Because I tend to blurt out what I want to say quickly, I tend to type that way as well. The advantage I have being online is that I can look at what I have typed and realize that I may have forgotten to include the niceties that should probably be included. I tend to just spit out the answer and forget to include the "Hi, how are you doing" stuff. By having the delay, it gives me the ability to edit what I want to say, so I can go back and add those things in later.

Netiquette

Being nice and adding those things are a part of what we call "tone" in the classroom. It is important to be polite and respectful toward your classmates and your instructors. People may often misinterpret your meaning, but by having time to edit and re-read what you have written, you can be sure that you are using an appropriate tone in all of your correspondence.

A word you will often hear that refers to how you should behave in an online classroom is "netiquette", a combination of "Internet" and "etiquette" – which is kind of cute. The rules for netiquette include the normal kinds of things involved in being polite, but there are some other things you should be aware of. For example, DO NOT TYPE IN ALL CAPS. Did you know that typing in all caps, like I just did, means you are yelling? Do not use a lot of abbreviations, either. Texting has done a number on how people type! It is not appropriate to write things like LMAO or LOL in online learning discussions. I see far too many students using slang, not capitalizing (where appropriate) and punctuating, and generally being inappropriate with disrespectful language when they are using online discussion rooms.

Emoticons

Many of you have probably used emoticons, which is the technical term for the little things like smiley faces that you can attach to emails and blogs. These used to be done with things like a colon followed by a closing bracket to signify a smiley face, but the latest software, which most schools have, offers the ability to insert an actual cartoon face. Although these can definitely be overused, they are sometimes a valuable tool you can use to let others know the intent behind what you are trying to say. If a phrase can be taken one of two ways, it may help to include a smiley face to show that the intent of the sender is positive. Remember not to over use them, though. It can be distracting to read a two sentence posting that has 10 emoticons flashing and smiling all over the place. I would reserve them just for those moments when they are really necessary to show intent. Try to keep them simple, as well. I have seen some where I have no idea what the face is supposed to be doing, and therefore the intent.

CHAPTER 9: WRITING SKILLS

"When asked, "How do you write?" I
invariably answer, "one word at a time."
~*Stephen King*

A lot of online students have been out of school for
a while. Because of this, they may be totally unaware
of the new guidelines that are out there for how papers
should look when they are submitted. Many schools require something called APA formatting. The good news
is, many schools do not require that you know how to
format your papers yet. They will teach you this in up-
coming courses. However, it is good to know what to
expect down the line.

What is APA?

APA stands for American Psychological Association.
This association has created rules that many schools
use as a format for how they want papers submitted.
There have been other formats such as MLA utilized in

the past, however I have found that most schools have now adopted APA standards, so I won't confuse you by explaining other formats. The APA manual is updated from time to time, and the most recent update, the sixth edition, occurred in 2009. The American Psychological Association Web site http://apastyle.apa.org/ provides tutorials and plenty of useful information. A lot of students find it helpful to see actual examples of what a paper should look like, and these can be viewed at http://my.ilstu.edu/~jhkahn/APAsample.pdf.   Another excellent source of information on APA formatting can be found at http://owl.english.purdue.edu/owl/resource/560/01/.

I took a long break between getting my masters and commencing my doctorate, and when I'd last attended school, a header was a term that I had only heard used in reference to cowboys and roping. Now, headers and footers are terms associated with the information that is included at the top or the bottom of every page when you are writing a paper. Although APA guidelines tell you what they expect in terms of margins, headers, etc., it does not tell you how to do these things within your Word document. There is an assumption that you know how to use word processing software. So, it is important that you know the basics about how to get around in Word so that you can do things like set up your margins and headers and generally be sure you are formatting your paper correctly.

Saving Files

The following examples using the most recent version of Word (2007), but it is important to note that previous versions of Word saved your documents with the file extension of ".doc". Word 2007 saves documents with a ".docx" extension. Students often try to get away with buying other, usually cheaper, software to do their homework, but always ensure that the software you purchase is appropriate for your school's requirements. For example, most schools no longer allow you to submit files that have a ".wps" extension, which is the file extension used by the Microsoft Works program.

You can see how your paper is being saved by typing a test paper. Open up Word and type a few lines. Now click on the "Office" button, the colorful icon at the top left of the screen. You will notice an option to "Save As". If you select that, it pulls up a screen that lets you name your document and decide where you want to save it to on your computer. Under the box where you type the name of your file, you will notice that there is a drop-down menu called "Save as type". If you are using Word 2007, your document will automatically be saved in ".docx" format. If you want to save it in ".doc" format, you need to select "Word 97-2003 document".

Formatting Your Paper

Now, using that same document, let's look at a few things that will make it easier for you later when the time comes to format your paper. You will notice that there are various toolbars and tabs like Home, Insert, Page Layout, References, Mailings, Review, View, etc. at the top of the page. Your document should be set on the Home tab when you open it up. If you look at the tool bar that is displayed under this tab on your screen, you will see that this is where you choose your font, align the text, etc. I will not go into too much detail here because I assume you have a basic understanding of this, however there are a few things that even experienced Word users may overlook.

Notice that on the toolbar there is a diagonal arrow in a little box in the bottom right corner of the various formatting areas, Clipboard, Font, Paragraph, and Styles. If you click on this arrow, it brings up another menu. Try it with the Font toolbar. Click on that arrow and notice how you can select Times New Roman font at 12 point size, for example. In the bottom left corner of this menu window there is a Default button. If you click on that, from this point onward, all of your papers will automatically display with the font settings you just chose. This is a very nice feature, because APA requires specific fonts, and it can be annoying to have to change the settings for every new document you create. If you now click on the arrow in the bottom right corner of the Paragraph area, you'll notice and item called Spacing, which is where you can choose your spacing between lines and before and after paragraphs. I have a lot of students who turn in papers with extra spaces between paragraphs. APA guidelines specify that you should not have any spaces between paragraphs, so be sure that the spacing before and after paragraphs is set to zero. If the default page that comes up when you first open Word inserts a space between paragraphs, as it often seems to do, you need to go to this area and change it to zero. Then, if you click on default, all your future papers will have this setting.

Another important area to understand is the Insert tab. If you click on this tab, you'll notice that it pulls up the area where you can set up your headers and page numbers. This is another requirement of APA formatting, so it is important to know where to find it. If you click on Header, it will show you examples of the options you can choose from. Be sure to set up your headers in the format required by APA. You will also need to be familiar with the page number area. APA formatting specifies page numbers in the upper right-hand corner of your page.

Another area to look at is the Page Layout tab. Remember our trick from before when we clicked on the little diagonal arrow at the bottom right corner of the toolbar? On this tab, the Page Setup toolbar has one of those as well. If you click on that, you will see the area where you can set up your margins. Again, once you've set up your margins, click on Default and your chosen settings will be retained for all future papers. Once you have your software set up with the correct margins, spacing, headers, etc., you are ready to type your papers.

Eventually, you will probably take a basic English course that will teach you how to write essays, but in the meantime it is simply good form, and will impress your professors, if you remember the basics of document structure. A good paper should have an introduction, a body, and a conclusion. It might be a good idea to freshen up your basic paragraph-structure skills.

Writing a Strong Paragraph

Here are some basic tips for a strong paragraph. Usually, the first line of a paragraph, which should be indented 5 spaces to meet APA requirements, is your topic sentence, and the rest of the paragraph pretty much just explains that sentence. Always ensure that you write suitably sized paragraphs. I see students who write very short paragraphs of only two or three lines, and I also see students who write a page or more for a single paragraph. Try to stay somewhere in the middle of those extremes. A good paragraph usually contains at least four or five sentences, which can vary in length, but it shouldn't take up an entire page. For more specifics about paragraph structure, check out http://lrs.ed.uiuc.edu/students/fwalters/para.html.

Proofreading

Remember to go over your paper before you submit it, proofreading and spell-checking your writing. Also be sure if you are starting in a master's level course or above, do not write in contractions such as can't or isn't. It is better to write cannot and is not. And do not forget to check out http://www.yourdictionary.com/library/misspelled.html for the correct spelling of challenging words.

CHAPTER 10: TEST TAKING

"I hate tests. It's a really lousy way to judge a person's ability."
~*Bill Paxton*

Like them or not, tests are probably here to stay. One thing you might be happy to hear though is that in online learning, there seems to be more papers to write than there are tests to take. For those of you who hate tests, this is good news. For those of you who hate writing papers, it may not be such good news. However, that is not to say there are no tests. Therefore it is critical to your success that your learn how to do your best when taking a test.

Technical Support

Be sure that if you have any difficulty while taking an online test, you contact technical support. Many students have had their computers lock up or their Internet connection drop out while they were in the middle of a test, but fear not. Technical support can usually get you back on track quickly, enabling you to complete the test on schedule.

Open-Book Tests

One really nice thing about taking online tests is that they are usually open-book format, which means you have your notes and texts available. However, that is not to say you have all the time in the world to look things up. Many of the tests that are given are timed, therefore if you are planning to refer to your notes, you need to be extremely organized, and know where to go for information quickly.

Preparing for the Test

Being good at taking tests has a lot to do with how much you prepare for the test. If you have a photographic memory and can cram everything you need into your brain on the night before the test is due to be taken, you are one lucky student. As for the rest of us, we need to make sure we plan our study time. If you have any questions about the material you are being tested on that haven't been answered sufficiently, you need to contact your instructor for further explanation. Go over the material you have covered, and any sample problems or notes you have taken. If it is an open-book test, try to create a one-page summary of all the key information on it that will either enable you to answer the questions or direct you to where you can find the necessary information quickly. As with any test, get a good night's sleep beforehand and eat well, so that you have plenty of energy and are thinking clearly.

Relieving Anxiety

If you are experiencing anxiety, there are a few things you can do to relieve it. The best thing is to know your material. The more you study, the more confidence you'll have and the less stressed you will feel. That is why it is not a good idea to cram the night before the test. When you commence the test, read the directions, take a quick look over the test to see what it includes, and then start with the easiest questions first, so that if you run out of time, at least you got to answer the questions you knew the answers to. This also gives you confidence to tackle the rest of the questions. If certain questions are worth more points than others, try to do the highest points-value questions early on as well. Try to stay focused on the question that is being asked, rather than worrying about how you will answer other questions. If you cannot come up with an answer immediately, skip that question and come back to it later. When you have finished the test, be sure to go over all your answers, double-checking that you've answered all the questions and that your answers are correct, to the best of your knowledge.

Types of Questions and How to Answer Them

Tests generally include one or more of the following types of questions: multiple choice, true/false, short answer, and essay. Occasionally, I have seen oral testing in doctoral courses but this is not a common test method, therefore we'll only cover the four types of test questions listed above.

Here are some helpful hints when taking a multiple choice test. As with any test, be sure you read the question carefully. Try not to look at the answers that are provided before you really know what the question is asking. Then, get rid of the answers you know are obviously incorrect right off the bat. That usually leaves you with two possible choices. Remember, your initial gut instinct is usually correct, so try not to second-guess yourself. Be careful with questions that offer "all of the above" or "none of the above" as one of the choices. If you notice that more than one answer has to be true, the answer is probably going to be "all of the above". Be careful about negatively worded questions, too. Sometimes you will see something like, "Which of the following does not occur?" Remember that you are looking for the thing that does *not* occur, rather than the thing that does occur. These types of questions can sometimes throw students off. Often, the correct answer to a question contains more wording than the other answers. This isn't always the case, but keep it in mind.

If the test you are taking is more essay-related, you should keep the following tips in mind. As with any question, read and reread the question until you are sure you understand exactly what is being asked. Be sure that your answer covers all the points that are required to fully answer the question. It's always better to include too much information rather than too little – but don't get carried away on one question and then find yourself running out of time. Remember to write in strong paragraphs. See the previous section on the correct formatting and structure for paragraph writing. Take your time answering questions, but keep any time limitations in mind. If the test consists of four essay questions and you only have an hour, try to move on to the next question after 15 minutes.

You don't see a lot of tests that are completely true/false these days. Usually, they are a combination of multiple choice, true/false, etc., however, when you do come across a true/false question and there is no penalty for guessing, it is better to offer some answer rather than nothing. After all you have a 50/50 chance of being correct. It is important to look for a negative format in this type of question, as well. Sometimes there are words like "never" or "always" that change the meaning of the question. If you see any part of the question that you know cannot possibly be true, then the answer should be "false".

For short-answer tests, remember, if the test is open-book, you can find the answers in your notes if you are well organized. It is always best to provide some answer, anything, rather than leaving it blank. If it is a math-related question, showing your working out is critical. Even if you come up with a wrong answer, sometimes the professor will see that at least you had the right idea.

CHAPTER 11: FUTURE PLANNING

"I arise in the morning torn between the desire to
improve the world and the desire to enjoy the world.
This makes it hard to plan the day."
~E. B. White

Where do you go from here? Perhaps you signed up for a class but had no idea what you were going to do after the first course. That happens. You may have a vague idea of getting an AA or a BS degree, but really aren't sure about which area you will pursue. It's important that you get to know your school counselor very well, because they can be an excellent resource for you during your time spent studying online. I have known a lot of counselors who have been a really big help for students who faced all kinds of dilemmas and needed someone to explain their options and help them make good decisions.

Career Choices or Continuing Education

Once you've taken a few classes, you may find that you have developed a particular interest in a topic that initially you had no idea you would like. If you do not have a career in mind, I would recommend reading "What Color is Your Parachute?" by Richard N. Bolles. It's updated regularly, and includes lots of information to help you find the type of career that best fits you, based on your interests and strengths.

Many students find that they want to continue online beyond their bachelor's degree, because many organizations are now looking for people with a master's degree. If you have learned how to get around online for a bachelor's degree, going on to get a master's is not that much different. It is just a higher level of study to further prepare you in your chosen field.

Having graduated with a degree, you are now in the market to get a better job. There are several sites out there where you can search for jobs using filters such as "Only look for jobs that require a degree." Some excellent sites for job hunting include Monster.com and Careerbuilder.com. If you're interested in going on to be an online instructor like me, you must have at least a master's degree. An excellent site to look for online teaching jobs is Higheredjobs.com. If you are going to be staying with your present employer, be sure to let them know that you have completed your degree.

Networking

You should also look into developing an ePortfolio, which is like an online résumé. What is nice about ePortfolios is that you can attach documents, images and audio/video clips. Another effective way of having your information easily available online is to set up your profile on a site like Linkedin.com. This is a very valuable networking site in that it shows your work history and information. It is also free, and the information can be viewed by those people you choose to get "linked in" with. You can create a public profile link and include it on your emails so that others can easily go to your site to find out more about you. To check out my linkedin public link, go to: http://www.linkedin.com/in/drdianehamilton.

Skills You Have Acquired

Be sure you update your résumé regularly to include new skills and qualifications you have acquired. Think of all the things you have learned from courses you have completed, including:

Critical and creative thinking
Writing
Quantitative learning
Seeing the big picture
Better goal setting
Better time management
Increased ability to read, take notes and take tests
Increased intelligence (IQ) and emotional intelligence
(EQ)

What is EQ?

These are all important skills. Often, schools require students to participate in group and team activities. Organizations like to know that their employees have learned these skills. Having to learn the information for your degree, you have increased your IQ. Having learned how to get along with your fellow classmates and have interpersonal relationships, you have also developed your EQ. Incidentally, companies are often now ranking EQ higher in importance than IQ. Having the ability to understand how others feel and to have empathy skills is an important personality trait that companies want to see in their leaders. If you are interested in learning more about emotional intelligence, I highly recommend Daniel Goleman's book "Emotional Intelligence: Why It Can Matter More Than IQ". I wrote my dissertation about how performance was impacted by having higher levels of EQ, and found that there was a correlation.

How Do You Eat An Elephant?

Online study is the future of learning. By choosing to undertake your degree online, it shows that you have taken the first step toward having a successful career. It is important that you then take the information you will have learned and utilize it to your best advantage. The longer you wait to start that first class, the longer it will be before you graduate. It may seem overwhelming at first, but it is just like anything else; the more you do it, the easier it becomes. I often have my online doctoral students ask me how they should begin such a major thing as writing a dissertation. I give them a corny answer, but one that is the truth. I say to them, "How do you eat an elephant?" The answer is, of course, "One bite at a time."

Online learning may someday replace face-to-face classroom learning entirely. Your children may not even know what a face-to-face classroom was like. As more and more students are finding themselves online, you will be in good company. One of the best things about learning online is the diversity of students in the classroom. You may have someone in the army overseas, you may have a fellow student in Australia, and you may have someone just down the street from you. You will certainly see a wide variety in terms of background, race, ethnicity and interests. Because there are a lot of discussion requirements in these classes, you will hear some interesting and, at times amazing stories. Online students often times have had extensive real-world experience, and are happy to share their insights with you. If you've had no work experience to date, don't worry; it's not a prerequisite. The nice thing is, the group will be so diverse that everyone will learn something from everybody else.

So, what are you waiting for? Online learning is waiting for you.

APPENDICES

Example Calendar

(If one is not provided by the professor, you can create your own similar to this.)

	Day 1	Day 2	Day 3	Day 4	Day 5	Day 6	Doy 7
Week 1							
	Post Bio		Assignment Due				Paper Due
	Remember to post at least X number of postings over X days during the week						
Week 2							
			Assignment Due				Paper Due
	Remember to post at least X number of postings over X days during the week						
Week 3							
			Assignment Due				Midterm Exam
	Remember to post at least X number of postings over X days during the week						
Week 4							
			Assignment Due				Paper Due
	Remember to post at least X number of postings over X days during the week						

Week 5							
			Assignment Due				Final Exam
	Remember to post at least X number of postings over X days during the week						

Example Syllabus

Prerequisites Teacher's Information Course Description	There are no prerequisites for this course. Teacher's bio may be posted here. This course will introduce students to XXXX concepts about the subject. Students will explore XXXX aspects about the subject. Some schools will list all assignments due here as well.
Course Objectives Or Out-comes	• Student will participate in discussions. • Student will write X number of expository essays on topics related to this course. • Student will be able to explain X topic. • Student will be able to compare and contrast X and X items. • Student will be able to distinguish between X and X.
Course Policies and Procedures	**Grading Criteria** Overall assessment for this course may be based on writings, discussion questions, essays, and quizzes.

50	Papers/Assignments
30	Discussion Online
20	Final

Grading Scale The grading scale for this class is pretty standard and straight forward:

A	90-100
B	80-89
C	70-79
D	60-69
F	Below 60

Late papers: Assignments will be marked 10% off for each day that they are late, up to a maximum of 4 days late. The final cannot be turned in after due date.

Plagiarism consists of using another author's words without proper identification and documentation. It is unacceptable.

Text-book(s)

Required: Text and Author

Example Rubric

(Each assignment will have certain points assigned to it. This gives you an example of what one assignment's requirements may be.)

Content 10 points	Points Earned XX/7
	Additional Comments:

• All topics are described in detail. • One example is given. • One source is given.	After grading the paper, the professor may write comments here.
Mechanics 3 Points	*Points Earned XX/3*
• The paper has an appropriate tone. • Complete sentences are used. • The spelling is correct.	Additional Comments: After grading the paper, the professor may write comments here.
Total 10 Points	*Points Earned XX/10*
Overall Comments:	The XX's will be filled in with your final grade after the professor has graded your paper.

Example Contact Information Sheet

Important Contacts	*Phone/Email/Best Hours to Reach Them*
Professor's Name: (Remember to list what they prefer to be called, i.e., Dr. or Mr. or Mrs., etc.)	Telephone Number: Email: Hours Available:
Academic Counselor/Advisor Name:	Telephone Number: Email: Hours Available:
Technical Support Number:	Telephone Number: Email: Hours Available:

Example Paper Setup

Basic set up for papers until you have learned proper APA formatting.

COVER PAGE

It is always a good idea to have a cover page. For an example of a cover page in an APA paper see http://my.ilstu.edu/~jhkahn/APAsample.pdf.

MARGINS

Margins at 1 inch (some schools require 1½ so be sure to check with your school). To set this up, in Word go to the Page layout tab and then on the page set up tool bar select Margins. If you select normal, it will set all sides to 1 inch.

SPACING

Double-space your document. In your Word document, click on the home tab, then on the Paragraph tool bar, click on the up and down arrow icon and choose 2.0.

PARAGRAPHS

Indent all paragraphs 5 spaces. Also be sure to write in standard-size paragraphs. A good-size paragraph is at least 4–5 sentences but should not be so long that it takes up an entire page. For more about writing a good paragraph, check out http://lrs.ed.uiuc.edu/students/fwalters/para.html.

SPACING BETWEEN PARAGRAPHS

Do not have extra spaces between paragraphs. The entire paper should simply be double-spaced. If your document defaults with an extra space between your paragraphs, go to the home tab, click on the Paragraph tool bar, then click the diagonal down arrow on the lower right corner. Be sure before and after spacing is set to zero. Click on Default so that it is set this way for future papers.

SPELL-CHECK

Be sure you spell-check all documents.

CITING/REFERENCES

Remember that if you cite, you will need to do so in proper APA formatting, which includes a reference page. See the following for example paper in APA: http://my.ilstu.edu/~jhkahn/APAsample.pdf . Notice how the reference page is set up on page 8 of that example.

STRUCTURE/FONTS

Be sure that papers are written with an introduction, body and conclusion. Also be sure you have your font set at 12 pt. – either Arial or Times New Roman. Always write in black font.

Problem/Issue Links

Problem or Issue	Where to go for help
Antivirus Software	www.norton.com or www. mcafee
APA Examples and Help	http://my.ilstu.edu/~jhk ahn/ APAsample.pdf or http:// owl.english.purd ue.edu/owl/ resource/560/01/ or http:// apastyle.apa.org/
Comparing Schools with Accreditation	www.AccreditedOnlin eCol- leges.com or http://www. elearners.com/ resources/agencies. asp
Grammar and Spelling Help	http://grammar.quickan ddirtytips.com/ or http:// www.yourdictionary.com/ library/misspe lled.html

Loan Information Or Grants	http://www.opm.gov/oca/pay/studentloan/html/fy05report.pdf or http://www.finaid.org/loans/publicservice.phtml or http://www.americorps. org or http://www.peacecorps. gov or http://www.friendsofvista.org or http://www.staffordloan.com/stafford-loan- info/ or http://www.college-scholarships-grants.biz/pell-grants-scholarships.shtml or http://www.tuitionpay.com/ or http://www.afford.com or http://www.fafsa.ed.gov/ or http://federalstudentaid.ed.gov/about/index.html or http://www.collegeboard.com/prod_downloads/about/news_info/trends/trends_aid_07.pdf or http://www.irs.gov/newsroom/article/0,,id=213 044,00.html or http://www.usnews.com/articles/education/paying-for-college/2010/02/18/will-you-get-enough-financial-aid-ask-your-college-about-these-10-factors.html
Networking	http://www.linkedin.com/in/drdianehamilton
Online Encyclopedia Personality Assessments	www.wikipedia.com

Personality Assessments	http://drdianehamilton.com/index.php?option=com_weblinks&view=category&id=39&Itemid=65
Study Techniques	http://www.studytechniques.org/reading-styles-strategies.html
Suggested Additional Reading	http://www.amazon.com/Emotional-Intelligence-10th-Anniversary-Matter/dp/055380491X/ref=sr_1_1?ie=UTF8&s=books&qid=1269127872&sr=8-1 or http://www.amazon.com/What-Color-Your-Parachute-2010/dp/1580089879/ref=sr_1_1?ie=UTF8&s=books&qid=1269129808&sr=8-1
Writing Help	http://lrs.ed.uiuc.edu/students/fwalters/para.html

Example Daily Activity Log

Time	List Your Activities	Time used wisely? Y/N
6:00 a.m.		
6:30 a.m.		
7:00 a.m.		
7:30 a.m.		
8:00 a.m.		
8:30 a.m.		
9:00 a.m.		
9:30 a.m.		
10:00 a.m.		
10:30 a.m.		
11:00 a.m.		
11:30 a.m.		
12:00 p.m.		
12:30 p.m.		
1:00 p.m.		
1:30 p.m.		
2:00 p.m.		

2:30 p.m.		
3:00 p.m.		
3:30 p.m.		
4:00 p.m.		
4:30 p.m.		
5:00 p.m.		
5:30 p.m.		
6:00 p.m.		
6:30 p.m.		
7:00 p.m.		
7:30 p.m.		
8:00 p.m.		
8:30 p.m.		
9:00 p.m.		
9:30 p.m.		

Example Personal SWOT Analysis

Strengths	Weaknesses
List all of the things that you see as strengths you possess that will allow you to be a successful online student and/or a successful employee. You may add more than 5 things but this will get you started. 1. 2. 3. 4. 5.	List all of the things that you see as weaknesses that could keep you from reaching your goals. Remember to also keep in mind solutions to these weaknesses that you may want to list under opportunities. 1. 2. 3. 4. 5.
Opportunities	Threats
List all of the things that you see as opportunities for you in your future, both personally and professionally. 1. 2. 3. 4. 5.	List all of the things that you see as possible threats to your success. Some of these things may be things like bad economic times, etc. 1. 2. 3. 4. 5.

Example Ways to Make a Good Impression

Important things to do to show you are a conscientious student.	Check off when completed
Be sure to respond to all questions asked of you by the instructor. Usually on the first day the instructor will send a welcome note. It is proper to respond to this, say hello, and show your enthusiasm for the course. If you prefer to be called a nickname, be sure you sign all of your postings with that name at the end to remind the professor.	
Submit your assignments early (if allowed). Remember to ask if it is allowable to submit early, if it is not stated anywhere. Discussion questions usually must be answered in the week that they are due, so it is not usually proper to answer them any earlier. You probably won't get credit for responding to prior week's discussion questions, so be sure you are responding to the proper week's discussion.	
Submit your assignments in APA format if required and/or you have already learned how to do it that way. It is usually not required for a first-time course. In such a preliminary course, you can usually apply a basic setup to your paper. See the example in the Appendix to make your papers stand out from the rest. This will show that you are very organized, and it will be easy for the instructor to read.	

Never write in any font other than 12-point Arial or Times New Roman. Always write in black. Do not write in **BOLD**, and do not write in *italic*.	
Capitalize first words of sentences. Always capitalize the word "I". Punctuate your sentences. Do not forget to use periods or commas.	
Never abbreviate or use acronyms or words like LOL, ROTFL, etc. Do not write like you would text. Write in complete sentences with words spelled out. Also write in complete paragraphs of at least 4–5 sentences if possible.	
Check your spelling. For example, "a lot" is two words and not one. Many students forget this. Do not write "alot"...it is "a lot".	
Never start a sentence with "Me". For example, "Me and Bob are going somewhere" is **not** correct. It should be "Bob and I are going somewhere". See http://grammar.quickanddirtytips.com/CategoryIndex/General_Grammar/page/1 for more help on grammar.	
Be sure you have a proper subject line on your postings. If you are posting a new thread or topic, be sure that you have a subject line that is relevant to what you are asking. For example, "Question on Assignment One from Diane Hamilton.	

Be sure you save your homework assignments with a name that makes it easy to locate, or in the form that is required by the instructor. For example, Hamilton-Week1Assn1 would be a good file name, so that the instructor can tell who submitted it and which assignment it is. Some instructors will tell you what to name your files. If they do, be sure you follow that format.

Keep track of how many discussion questions or participation postings are required per week.

Example Word Default Settings

How to set up your Word document's default settings.

FONT

In your open Word document click on the home tab at the top of the page. Click on the downward diagonal arrow at the bottom right corner next to the word Font. Choose Times New Roman 12 point, and be sure the font color is set to black or automatic. The font style should be set on regular, and not on bold or italic. Click the Default button. When it asks if you want to have this setting for all future documents, answer "Yes".

MARGINS

In your open Word document click on the Page Layout tab at the top of the page. Click on the downward diagonal arrow at the bottom right corner next to the words Page Setup. Make sure the top, bottom, left and right settings are all at 1 inch. Click the Default button. When it asks if you want to have this setting for all future documents, answer "Yes".

SPACING

In your open Word document click on the Page Layout tab at the top of the page. Click on the downward diagonal arrow at the bottom right corner next to the word Paragraph. Be sure that the settings for before and after paragraphs are both set at zero. Click the Default button. When it asks if you want to have this setting for all future documents, answer "Yes".

HEADERS

A header is like a title for your paper. Some professors may require you to include this. I do not recommend having a header automatically set up for all of your Word documents. It is probably better to do this on an assignment-by-assignment basis. In your open Word document click on the Insert tab at the top of the page. Click on the Word Header and then choose "blank". It will then let you type in your header. If you want to have the header on the right side of the screen, you can then click on the home tab and choose the left adjustment setting on the paragraph tab. If you want to remove the header, you can backspace through it. If you ever want to close out of the header function, click on the word "header" on the top left of your typed paper.

PAGE NUMBERING

I do not recommend having page numbering automatically set up for all of your Word documents. It is better to do this on an assignment-by-assignment basis. In your open Word document click on the Insert tab at the top of the page. Click on the Page Numbering feature. Choose "Top of Page" and then the option where the page number is on the right side (called Plain number 3). If you change your mind and want the number removed, just backspace through it and then close that screen. To close out of the numbering function, click on the word "header" on the top left of your typed paper.

Example Personality Study Techniques

Studying based on your personality type – where to go for more information.

Verbal-Linguistic – If you do well taking notes and listening to lectures, you may be a Verbal-Linguistic learner. For more information about this, check out http://learningdisabilities. about.com/od/resourcesresearch/qt/visual_learner.htm and http://www.ldpride.net/learningstyles.MI.htm#Verbal/ Linguistic%20Intelligence.

Logical-Mathematical – If you do well with reasoning and numbers, you may be a Logical-Mathematical learner. For more information about this, check out http://www. learning-styles-online.com/style/logical-mathematical/ and http://www.ldpride.net/learningstyles.MI.htm#Verbal/Lingui stic%20Intelligence.

Bodily-Kinesthetic – If you do well with balance and eye-hand coordination, you may be a Bodily-Kinesthetic learner. For more information about this, check out http:// learningdisabilities.about.com/od/resourcesresearch/qt/ Bodily_kinesthe.htm and http://www.ldpride.net/learning-styles.MI.htm#Verbal/Lingui stic%20Intelligence.

Visual-Spatial – If you do well with learning through pictures, maps and charts, you may be a Visual-Spatial learner. For more information about this, check out http://www. learning-styles-online.com/style/visual-spatial/ and http:// www.ldpride.net/learningstyles.MI.htm#Verbal/Lingui stic%20Intelligence.

Interpersonal – If you do well interrelating with others through discussion and debate, you may be an interpersonal learner. For more information about this, check out http:// www.learning-styles-online.com/style/social- interpersonal/ and http://www.ldpride.net/learningstyles.MI.htm#Verbal/ Lingui stic%20Intelligence.

Intrapersonal – If you do well at understanding your own emotions and motivations, you may be an intrapersonal learner. For more information about this, check out http://www.learning-styles-online.com/style/solitary-intrapersonal/ and http://www.ldpride.net/learningstyles.MI.htm#Verbal/Linguistic%20Intelligence.

Musical – If you do well at learning through memo rizing and using songs, you might be a musical learner. For more information about this, check out http://www.learning-styles-online.com/style/aural-auditory-musical/ and http://www.ldpride.net/learningstyles.MI.htm#Verbal/Linguistic%20Intelligence.

Naturalistic – If you do well at learning through utilizing patterns or you enjoy science, you might be a naturalistic learner. For more information about this, check out http://www.personal.psu.edu/bxb11/MI/MITypes.htm.

REFERENCES

AccreditedOnlineColleges.com (2010). Retrieved from www.accreditedonlinecolleges.com on March 19, 2010.

Allen, David (2002). Getting Things Done. Penguin Books. New York.

APAStyle.org. (2010). Retrieved from http://apastyle. apa.org/ on March 19, 2010.

Bear & Nixon (2006). Bears Guide to Earning Degrees by Distance Learning, Ten Speed Press, Toronto.

Careerbuilder.com (2010). Retrieved from www.career-builder.com on March 19, 2010.

Chariho.k12.ri.us (2010). Retrieved from www.chariho. k12.ri.us on March 19, 2010.

Collegeboard.com (2010). Retrieved from http://www. collegeboard.com/prod_downloads/about/news_ info/trends/trends_aid_07.pdf on March 19, 2010.

Colleges-Scholarships-Grants.biz (2010). Retrieved from http://www.college-scholarships-grants.biz/pell-grants-scholarships.shtml on March 19, 2010.

eLearners.com (2010). Retrieved from www.elearners. com on March 19, 2010.

FAFSA.ed.gov (2010). Retrieved from http://www.fafsa.ed.gov/ on March 19, 2010.

Federalstudentaid.ed.gov (2010). Retrieved from http://federalstudentaid.ed.gov/about/index.html on March 19, 2010.

Finaid.org (2010). retrieved from http://www.finaid.org/loans/publicservice.phtml on March 19, 2010.

FLDCU.org/online-traditional (2010). Retrieved from www.fldcu.org/online-traditional on March 19, 2010.

Goleman, Daniel (2006). Emotional Intelligence: Why it Can Matter More Than IQ, Bantam Books, New York.

GrammarGirl.com (2010). Retrieved from http://grammar.quickanddirtytips.com/ on March 19, 2010.

IDPride.net (2010). Retrieved from www.IDpride.net on March 19, 2010.

IRS.gov (2010). Retrieved from http://www.irs.gov/newsroom/article/0,,id=213044,00.html on March 19, 2010.

Lakein, Alan (1974). How to Get Control of Your Time and Your Life, Penguin Books, London, England.

LRS.ed (2010). Retrieved from http://lrs.ed.uiuc.edu/students/fwalters/para.html on March 19, 2010.

Myllstu.edu (2010). Retrieved from http://my.ilstu.edu/~jhkahn/APAsample.pdf on March 19, 2010.

NCES.ed.gov (2010). Retrieved from www.nces.ed.gov on March 19, 2010.

OPM.gov (2010). Retrieved from http://www.opm.gov/oca/pay/studentloan/html/fy05report.pdf on March 19, 2010.

Owl.English.purdue.edu (2010). Retrieved from http://owl.english.purdue.edu/owl/resource/560/01/ on March 19, 2010.

Phoenix.edu (2010). Retrieved from http://www.phoenix.edu/students/how-it-works/innovative_education_technology/computer_requirements.html on March 19, 2010.

Sloan Consortium (2010). Retrieved from http://www.sloan-c.org on March 19, 2010.

Staffordloan.com (2010). Retrieved from http://www.staffordloan.com/stafford-loan-info/ on March 19, 2010.

StudyTechniques.com (2010). Retrieved from http://www.studytechniques.org/reading-styles-strategies.html on March 19, 2010.

SuccessDegrees.com (2010). Retrieved from http://www.successdegrees.com/costofonlinecollegecourses.html on March 19, 2010.

U.S. Department of Education (2009). Retrieved from http://www2.ed.gov/rschstat/eval/tech/evidence-based-practices/finalreport.pdf on March 19, 2010.

U. S. News and World Report (2010). Retrieved from http://www.usnews.com/articles/education/paying-for-college/2010/02/18/will-you-get-enough-financial-aid-ask-your-college-about-these-10-factors.html on March 19, 2010.

Wikipedia.com (2010). Retrieved from www.wikipedia.com on March 19, 2010.

YourDictionary.com (2010). Retrieved from http://www.yourdictionary.com/library/misspelled.html on March 19, 2010.

GLOSSARY

Accreditation – Quality of the education provided meets the U.S. Dept. of Education standards. There are nationally recognized agencies that the U.S. Dept. of Education recognizes that accredit universities.

ACT – American College Testing Program – test given to high school students to measure education and ability to do well in college.

Advisor – Advisors or counselors help students choose classes and set schedules. They give advice on things other than homework-related items that deal with how to be successful in school.

APA Format – American Psychological Association Format is a guide for formatting students' papers, including how margins, fonts, citations, etc. should look.

Associate Degree – Usually a two-year college-level degree.

Asynchronous – Not at the same time. In college courses, if a course is asynchronous it means that everybody does not have to participate at the same time.

Attaching Files – When submitting assignments, attaching or uploading is similar to sending an email with an attachment or an uploaded file.

Attendance – Usually a student is considered in attendance on any given day should they post anything to any area of the classroom to show they were there.

Bachelorette – Academic degree, usually four years in length.

Blackboard – Software that many schools use to access the classroom.

Bodily-Kinesthetic Intelligence – Learners express themselves through movement.

Chat Room – An area in the online classroom where students can talk about things as if they were in a hallway or relaxation area in a regular school. Topics must be clean but do not have to be related to the course.

Correspondence Course – School course taken though regular mail or sometimes through email.

Counselor – See Advisor

Critical thinking – According to the Foundation for Critical Thinking (2010), critical thinking is the intellectually disciplined process of actively and skillfully conceptualizing, applying, analyzing, synthesizing, and/or evaluating information gathered from, or generated by, observation, experience, reflection, reasoning, or communication, as a guide to belief and action.

Cum Laude – With distinction.

Curriculum – Educational courses offered.

Day timer – Planner, usually with calendar.

Diploma Mill – A higher-education institution that gives diplomas based on less-than-quality education for a financial return.

Discussion Board – Area in the online classroom where students post responses to questions posted by the professor.

Distance Education – Education that is not necessarily delivered in the same location, as in a traditional classroom.

Doc Share – An area within the software program eCollege where students can upload their documents so that others within the course can see and respond to them.

Doctoral Degree – One of the highest degrees offered by a university, for example a Ph.D.

Dropbox – An area within the software program eCollege where students can upload their documents so that only the professor can see them.

eCollege – An online learning software platform used by colleges.

E-Learning – Online education.

Emoticons – A group of characters used to convey intended tone, e.g. a smiley face :).

Emotional Intelligence – The ability to understand one's emotions as well as the emotions in others.

Emotional Quotient or EQ – The measure of one's emotional intelligence, similar to how IQ measures regular intelligence.

e-Portfolio – An electronic way to assemble a collection of work you have done, including writings, pictures, blogs, etc.

Essay – A written paper.

Extension – In software, the extension is the part of the filename that comes after the period. For example, if a file is named "Sample.doc" then the extension is ".doc".

Extrovert – Someone who prefers to think and process information externally.

Feedback Area – An area in software platforms such as Blackboard where students can see input from the instructor as to how they are doing in the class.

Footer – The area at the bottom of a document where details such as page numbers, etc. may go.

Font – The typeface that is chosen for a document.

Forum – An area within certain software packages such as OLS, which is like a classroom or place that a student will go to find information.

Grade Scale – Explanation for what percentages equivocate to certain grades. For example, 90% may be an A, 80% a B, and so on.

Grammar – The study of the preferred way to write words.

Grant – A way to finance your education, unlike loans in the fact that they do not have to be paid back.

Header – The area at the top of your paper where you might include details such as page numbers or other information about the assignment.

Incomplete – A student may request a grade of incomplete should they have an emergency and not be able to complete the course in time. This usually includes an extended amount of time to finish the course and is up to the professor's discretion.

Interpersonal Intelligence – The ability to understand others.

Intrapersonal Intelligence – The ability to understand yourself.

Introvert – A person who prefers to think or process information internally.

IQ – Measure of intelligence.

Logical-Mathematical Intelligence – Prefers to think with logic, reasoning and numbers.

Magna Cum Laude – Graduating with high honors.

Masters – Next degree level after receiving a bachelor's degree.

Mentor – A person of trust to guide you. Usually someone who has more experience than you do in an area where they help you learn.

MLA – Modern Language Association. A style of writing that schools may use. Most commonly, they use APA.

Myers Briggs – A mother-daughter team who created the Myers–Briggs Assessment to study personality preferences.

Musical Intelligence – When music and hearing help with learning, a student is said to have musical intelligence.

Naturalistic Intelligence – When being around outdoors, plants and animals helps with learning, a student is said to have naturalistic intelligence.

Netiquette – Combination of "Internet" and "etiquette", meaning how to behave properly and not be rude in the online environment.

OLS – Online Learning System software offered by universities to allow students to access their online classes.

Online Learning – Ability to learn or take courses through the use of computers rather than having to attend a brick-and-mortar classroom.

Participation – Posting something of substance in a course, usually in response to discussion questions posted by the instructor. Unlike attendance, there must be quality to the posting.

Peer-Reviewed – Peers of the writer of an article have reviewed the document.

Plagiarism – Taking someone else's work and trying to submit it as your own.

Platform – Software that universities use for online courses to enable students to have access to classes.

Post-Secondary Education – Education that occurs after high school, e.g. college.

Procrastination – Putting off until tomorrow what you can do today.

Retention – The ability to retain or remember things.

Rubric – Rules for how one will be graded.

SAT – Scholastic Aptitude Test given to high school students to assess intelligence and readiness for college.

Search Engine – Software that searches the Internet for specific things. Examples include Google, Yahoo and Bing. Educational examples include ProQuest and EBSCOhost.

SQ3R – Stands for Survey, Question, Read, Recite and Review. It is a process that students can use to study and have better retention.

Syllabus – A summary of course requirements or expectations.

Synchronous – Attending class at the same time as your fellow students and instructors.

Technical Support – The help-desk people you call when you are having computer-related problems with online courses.

Thread – A posting in class where students and the professor continue a conversation.

TOEFL – Test of English as a Foreign Language – Test to evaluate English skills.

TurnItIn – A software platform that colleges often use to test students' papers for plagiarism.

Uploading Files – See attaching files.

Verbal-Linguistic Intelligence – When spoken or written words help students learn better they are said to have verbal-linguistic intelligence.

Virtual University – An online university.

Visual-Spatial Intelligence – When pictures or visual aids help students learn better they are said to have visual-spatial intelligence.

Wiki – A software platform that allows multiple users to input information.

Wikipedia – An online encyclopedia site where students can go to discover basic information. It is important to note is that this is a good place to start looking for information, but not a good source to use when you start to cite references. Because it is a wiki (see definition for wiki), the information on it can be manipulated by numerous users, and therefore can be unreliable.

YouTube – A Web site where videos are uploaded. Some schools include links to lectures or other items on the site.

INDEX

ABOUT THE AUTHOR

Diane Hamilton has a Doctorate Degree in Business Management. She currently teaches bachelor-, master-, and doctoral-level courses for six online universities. Along with her teaching experience, she has more than twenty-five years of business and management-related experience. Her background includes work in many industries, including computers, software, pharmaceuticals, corporate training, mortgage/lending, and real estate. After many years of teaching online students, Dr. Hamilton discovered there was a need for developing basic life skills in young adults. Her books and articles focus on understanding online education, personalities in the workforce, and personal finance. She lives in Arizona, is married to Robert Spies, MD, and has two grown daughters, Terra and Toni. She and Toni are co-authoring a book on personalities.

12683311R00105

Made in the USA
Lexington, KY
19 December 2011